Building The Six-Hour Canoe is a wonderful way to get afloat. Quickly and simply built, the Six-Hour Canoe is suitable for builders and paddlers young and old.

The Six-Hour Canoe is the brainchild of Mike O' ⟦...⟧ **WoodenBoat** Publications and Publisher of **Boat Desi** ⟦...⟧ ⟦designed as an easily built and inexpensive boat f⟧ students, it has been adapted by the Center for Water⟦...⟧ purpose vehicle. Suitable as a personal boat - light and easy to carry and handle - it is also an ideal boat for introductory boat building courses and for community and school based boat building experiences. Many of these boats have been built by fifth and sixth graders.

Inexpensive to build, using common tools and materials, it can give almost anybody access to boat building and to a boat. The Six-Hour Canoe is constructed from a single 4' x 16' sheet of marine plywood and a few pieces of dimensional lumber. When constructed with epoxy glued seams, it remains leak free from the moment it is put in the water.

In this book are the designer's plans and detailed building instructions.. You can use them directly in building your own Six-Hour Canoe. As the designer says, "Nothing, absolutely nothing, conveys the joy of being afloat quite so purely as a light paddling boat." Build your own Six-Hour Canoe and find out for yourself....

"Thousands of folks have built this Mike O'Brien-designed double-paddle canoe using this very book. Detailed Instructions combined with a simple process make for a weekend boatbuilding project, and years of paddling." **WoodenBoat**

"One Weekend-One Canoe. It's light, it's fast, it's agile, and for two days work and less than $150, it will take you anywhere there's water." **Outdoor Life**

About the authors:

William Bartoo, Richard Butz and John Montague founded the Watercraft Studies program at Buffalo State College in Buffalo, New York. Beginning with the building of a single kayak in a survey course in wood design, the program has grown to include an academic minor, research in historic craft indigenous to the eastern Great Lakes and ever expanding community and public school boatbuilding projects.

While all three authors have been involved in boats and boat building for many years, it was only in 1989 that they officially started the watercraft courses at the college.

Bartoo, a furniture designer by training, oversaw the boat design and construction projects. He is now on the Benford Design Group staff. Montague, a design historian, built a Caledonia yawl boat and is primarily responsible for the historic research and archival activities of the program. Butz, a potter and administrator, is currently working on several Adirondack guideboats and administers watercraft studies activities. In addition to being on faculty, they teach boat building courses, lecture outside the college, conduct workshops in boat building and consult on community and public school partnerships.

The authors, clockwise from left, William Bartoo, John Montague and Richard Butz.

Building
The Six-Hour Canoe

Designed By Mike O'Brien
Text By Richard Butz
Illustrations By John Montague
Lines Plans Drawings By William Bartoo

Tiller Publishing

St. Michaels, MD 21663
(410) 745-3750

Layout and design by Tiller Publishing.

Photos supplied by the authors, except as noted.

Tiller Publishing

St. Michaels, MD 21663
Voice: 410-745-3750
Fax: 410-745-9743

TABLE OF CONTENTS

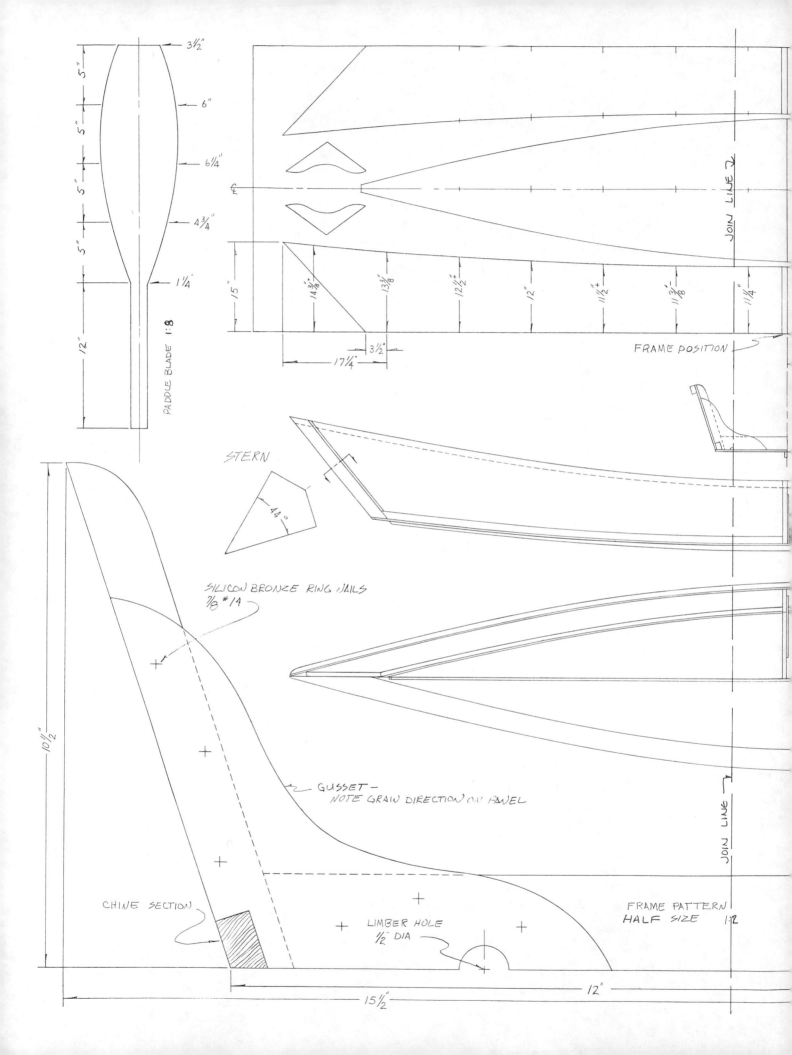

PADDLE BLADE 1:8

3½"
5"
5"
6"
5"
5"
6¼"
5"
4¾"
5"
1¼"
12"

JOIN LINE 2

15"
14⅜"
13⅜"
12½"
12"
11½"
11⅜"
11¼"
3½"
17¼"

FRAME POSITION

STERN

44°

SILICON BRONZE RING NAILS
⅞ #14

GUSSET—
NOTE GRAIN DIRECTION ON PANEL

10½"

CHINE SECTION

LIMBER HOLE
½" DIA

JOIN LINE

FRAME PATTERN
HALF SIZE 1:2

12"

15½"

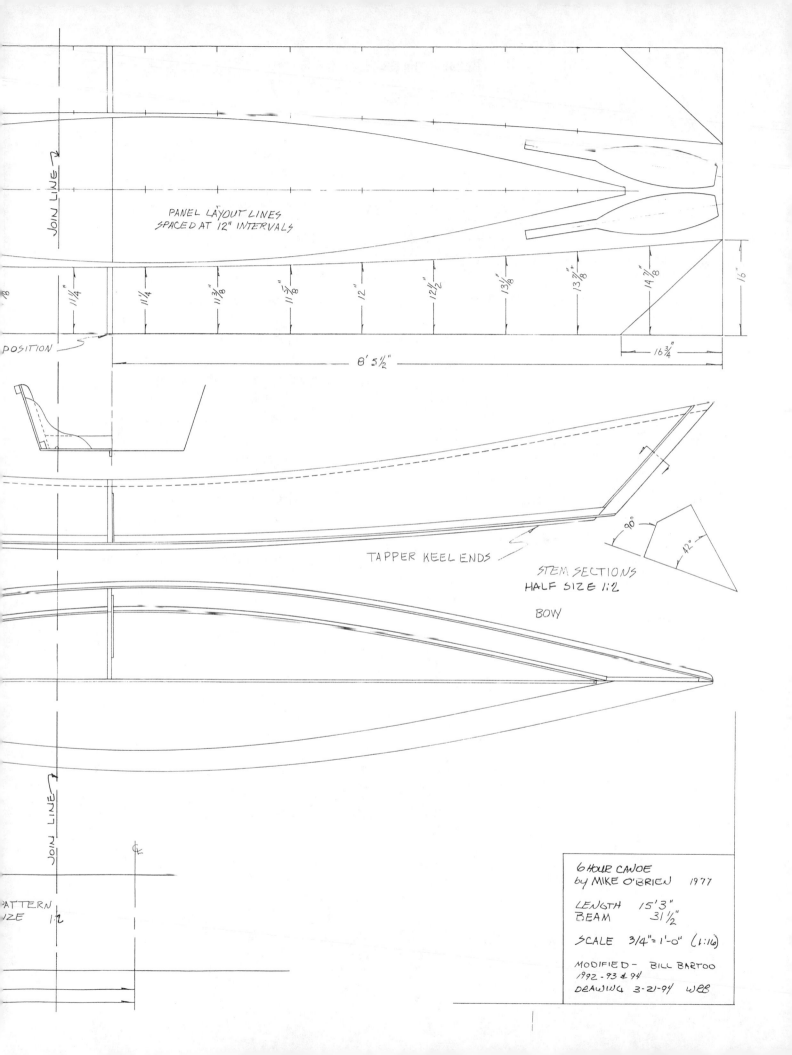

JOIN LINE

PANEL LAYOUT LINES
SPACED AT 12" INTERVALS

1/8"

POSITION

11 1/4"   11 1/4"   11 3/8"   11 5/8"   12"   12 1/2"   13 3/8"   13 7/8"   14 7/8"   16"

8' 5 1/2"

16 3/4"

TAPPER KEEL ENDS

STEM SECTIONS
HALF SIZE 1:2

BOW

90°   42°

JOIN LINE

℄

PATTERN
SIZE 1:2

6 HOUR CANOE
by MIKE O'BRIEN   1977

LENGTH   15' 3"
BEAM   31 1/2"

SCALE 3/4" = 1'-0" (1:16)

MODIFIED - BILL BARTOO
1992 - 93 + 94
DRAWING 3-21-94   WBB

DESIGNER'S INTRODUCTION

by Mike O'Brien

In 1977, near the end of a hazy August afternoon, I stood at the door to my boat shop contemplating the fate of two perfect sheets of 1/4" Bruynzeel mahogany plywood. They were survivors of a 56-sheet order, most of which had found its way into a cruising sailboat. I devised this double-paddle canoe as being a quick and pleasant end for the leftovers.

The canoe went together quickly (as the name implies), and it remains alive and well as I write this in the spring of 1994. Through the years it has given pleasure far beyond the market value of two pieces of plywood and six hours of building time. With the paddle sitting idly in my hands, I've drifted through long afternoons in shallow Chesapeake coves. Six inches below, the life struggle of the bottom community played out like a movie. I've rested in these same coves on autumn evenings and watched silently as Canada geese crossed the moon and came down to sleep.

Pulling myself along by grabbing the underbrush on each bank, I've worked this simple canoe far up into streams of the New Jersey Pine Barrens — under disused bridges that haven't connected passable roads for half a century, and past long-collapsed homesteads marked only by aging ornamental trees.

Nothing, absolutely nothing, conveys the joy of being afloat quite so purely as a light paddling boat.

PART I

BUILDING THE SIX-HOUR CANOE

The Six-Hour Canoe is the brainchild of Mike O'Brien, Senior Editor at **WoodenBoat** Publications and Publisher of **Boat Design Quarterly**. Originally designed as an easily built and inexpensive boat for use by oceanography students, it has been adapted by the Center for Watercraft Studies as a multi-purpose vehicle. Suitable as a personal boat - light and easy to carry and handle - it is also an ideal boat for introductory boat building courses and for community and school based boat building experiences. We have built many of these boats with fifth and sixth graders.

Inexpensive to build, using common tools and materials, it can give almost anybody access to boat building and to a boat. The Six-Hour Canoe is constructed from a single 4' x 16' sheet of marine plywood and a few pieces of dimensional lumber. When constructed with epoxy glued seams, it remains leak free from the moment it is put in the water.

Application

The maximum safe load is about 250 lbs., making the boat suitable for one adult or several children. It is designed for sheltered waters and should not be used in rough conditions or in swift rivers. Its real application is in quiet ponds or lakes where its shallow draft makes it ideal for exploring.

How to Use This Manual

In writing a manual such as this, we have had to build the boat in our heads. And the problem with that approach is similar to building a boat in your basement - when it's finished you hope you can get it out the door. We hope we can offer clear enough explanations and drawings so you can get the boat out of our heads and into the water.

Read the manual carefully, all the way through, and try to picture the sequence. We assume no prior boat building experience but we do assume your ability to follow directions and to learn how to handle simple tools.

Take your time and enjoy the process. John Gardner, the noted boat builder, author of many books on the subject and Curator Emeritus at the Mystic Seaport Museum, urges the builder to have a comfortable chair nearby when building a boat. It's good advice. You can sit in your chair and think things through or just enjoy the progress you've made. We recommend it.

Preparations

A materials and tools list follows and all materials and tools should be assembled before proceeding. Hand tools are adequate and even desirable for most of the construction process, providing blades are sharp. However, a band saw would be most useful in cutting out the stems.

The boat is fifteen feet long and you will need an adequate place in which to build it. On clear and temperate days the process can be moved outside.

Safety

When using hand or power tools it is essential that the user read and understand instruction manuals and observe proper safety procedures. Local lumber yards can often provide milling and cutting services, eliminating the need to use unfamiliar power tools.

Sections

This manual is organized in sequential sections. They are:

1   Assembly of materials and tools
2   The plans and how to use them
3   Laying out and cutting the side and bottom panels
4   Laying out and cutting the stems
5   Laying out and cutting the gussets
6   Milling the stock for the frame, gunwales, and chine logs
7   Assembling the frame
8   Attaching the stems
9   Attaching the frame
10 Closing in the side panels
11 Cutting, installing and planing the chine logs
12 Cutting and installing the gunwales
13 Cutting and attaching the bottom
14 Trimming the bottom and sheer
15 Sanding and finishing
16 Deck options
17 Flotation options
18 Seating options
19 Keels
20 Final thoughts

Section 1. Assembling the Materials and Tools

The materials and tools list is in appendix "A". However, some thought should be given to the kinds of materials that can be used. The hull materials are:

(See Butt Block Option in Appendix C)

1 pc.	1/4" x 4' x 16' marine plywood
2 pcs.	3/4" x 1-1/2" x 14' pine or spruce (chine logs)
2 pcs.	3/4" x 1 1/2" x 16' pine or spruce (gunwales)
1 pc.	3/4" x 2" x 3' pine or spruce (frame bottom)
2 pcs.	3/4" x 1 1/2" x 11" pine or spruce (frame sides)
2 pcs.	2" x 4" x 28" pine or spruce stem pieces
1 lb.	7/8" bronze ring nails
50	3/4" #8 bronze screws
1 lb.	3/4" drywall screws
1 qt.	marine epoxy glue assorted finishes

Plywood

The boat is constructed out of a single sheet of marine plywood sixteen feet long. For the amateur builder it is probably best to purchase the 16' panel instead of "scarfing" (joining) two 4' x 8' panels. It is important that a marine plywood be used because of its suitability for wet conditions.

Dimensional Lumber

The dimensional lumber should all be knot free. This is particularly true of the chine logs and gunwales which will have to bend around the curve of the boat. Pine and spruce are used because they are easily obtained and are easy to cut and plane.

Fastenings

The boat can be put together with no mechanical fastenings at all. That is, it can be temporarily clamped or held with drywall screws until the epoxy sets. However, most people prefer to use bronze ring nails to hold the stems, chine logs and bottom, and bronze screws for the frame and gunwales.

Various kinds of marine epoxy glues are available and directions should be followed in detail for best results. Always wear protective gloves and safety glasses when using epoxy to avoid skin or eye irritation. And, be sure to use ample epoxy so you have some "squeeze out" when clamping or fastening. "Starving a joint" can result in the pieces coming apart.

Finishes

The Six-Hour Canoe can be finished with a primer and single coat of paint or it can be given the "yacht treatment", complete with varnish and marine enamels. Good results have been obtained with a simple exterior paint such as Sears Latex Weatherbeater over an oil based exterior primer.

Tools

The tools list covers the tools that are necessary and those that are optional. The instructions will suggest appropriate tools as needed. Again, be sure to follow all safety procedures when using hand and power tools.

Other Supplies

Duct tape
Acid brushes for epoxy
Cups for mixing epoxy
Rubber gloves
1 lb. 3/4" #6 or #8 dry wall or deck screws (for temporary fastening)

Panel Measurements:
Computer calculated for sheer only, measured in decimal inches and then converted.

Station No.	Position	Height	Height nearest 1/16"	Height nearest 1/8"
1	00.00	16.00	16	16
2	12.00	14.89	14 7/8	14 7/8
3	24.00	13.92	13 15/16	13 7/8+
4	36.00	13.12	13 1/8	13 1/8
5	48.00	12.49	12 1/2	12 1/2
6	60.00	11.99	12	12
7	72.00	11.64	11 5/8	11 5/8
8	84.00	11.39	11 3/8	11 3/8
9	96.00	11.26	11 1/4	11 1/4
10	108.00	11.23	11 1/4	11 1/4
11	120.00	11.32	11 5/16	11 3/8-
12	132.00	11.56	11 9/16	11 1/2+
13	144.00	11.97	12	12
14	156.00	12.56	12 9/16	12 1/2+
15	168.00	13.38	13 3/8	13 3/8
16	180.00	14.42	14 7/16	14 3/8+
17	185.25	15.00	15	15

Section 2. The Plans and How to Use Them

The plans give the dimensions of all the pieces in the boat. In addition there are patterns for the stems, the frame gussets and for the frame, itself. Read the plans thoroughly and identify the various parts.

Be sure to check and double check when you transfer dimensions from the plans to the panel or stock. Always mark each piece after you lay it out and mark the position of stems and frame on the side panels and bottom. Identify and mark bow and stern sections on the side panels and mark the bow and stern stem pieces so as not to mismatch during the gluing process.

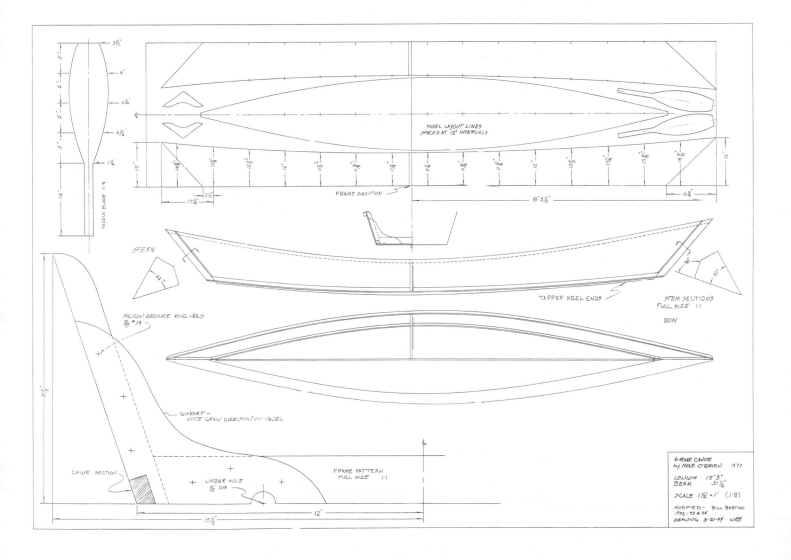

Section 3. Laying Out and Cutting the Side and Bottom Panels

Mark a centerline lengthwise down the center of both sides of your plywood panel.

Mark one end of your plywood panel as the bow end. Working from the end, mark lines across the panel at 12" intervals, beginning from the bow - these will be your layout lines.

To locate the frame position measure 8' 5 1/2" from the bow. Draw a line across the panel and another, aft and parallel to it, 3/4" from the first. This will mark the position of the frame on both the side and bottom panels. Turn the panel over and mark these two lines on the other side.

Return to the first side and mark the angles of the bow and stern as shown on the plans.

At the frame lines, measure 11 1/4" from the edge of the panel and make a mark. Drive a finishing nail part-way in at these marks. Do this at each side of the panel. Drive finishing nails part-way in at the tips of the bow and stern on each side as shown.

Stretch a batten (a long straight piece of wood 1" x 1") along the panel as shown, making a line that connects the bow and stern, curving through the 11 1/4" frame line marks. This will become your sheer line. (The sheer line is the top edge of the sides.) Draw a line along the batten, as the illustration shows. Repeat on the other side.

Note: If you do not have a batten, you can use one of your gunwales, turned up on its side so it will spring, easily, along the sheer line.

Cutting Out:

Using an electric saber saw or a hand saw, cut out the side panels. Cut about 1/8" outside the line.

After the panels are cut out, clamp the two side panels together and plane to the lines, using a block plane.

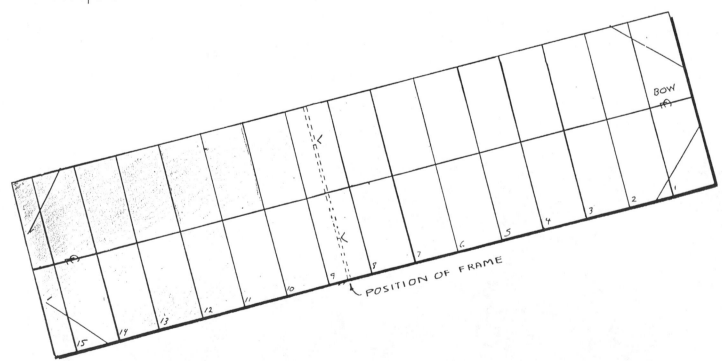

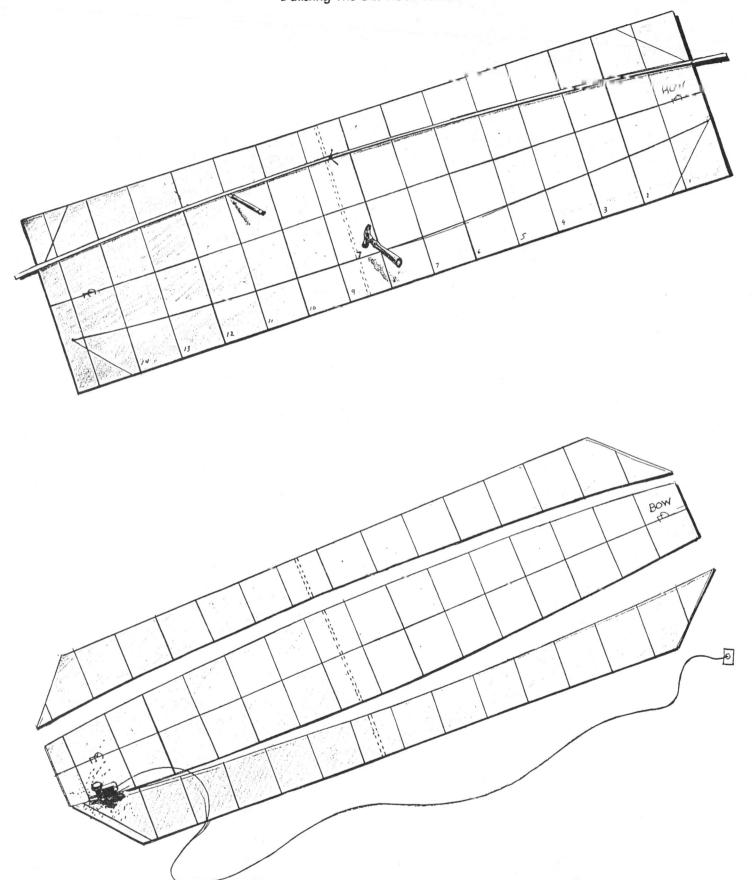

Section 4. Laying Out and Cutting the Stems

The stem pieces form the proper angles at the bow and stern and the side panels are attached to them. It is important that these angles be correct.

Using the 2 x 4's and the patterns for the bow and stern stem pieces, mark out the lines of the patterns on the ends of the appropriate stem stock. There are several options at this point:

Option 1 -

a.   Tilt the table of a band saw and attach a fence as shown and cut the stems out. Remember, the bow and stern angles are slightly different so the angle of the table must be adjusted for each stem. (68° Bow 66° Stern)

b.   After the stems are cut, return the table of the band saw to 90° and cut as shown. Or you can use a table saw for this process.

Option 2 -

Draw a line connecting the vertices of the triangles and hand plane the stems as shown.

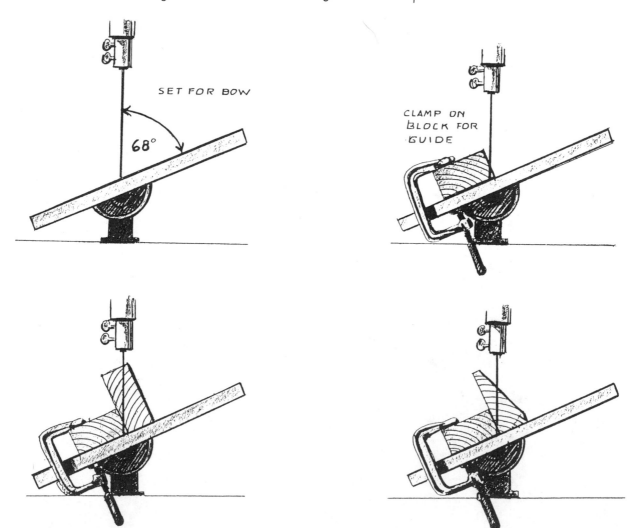

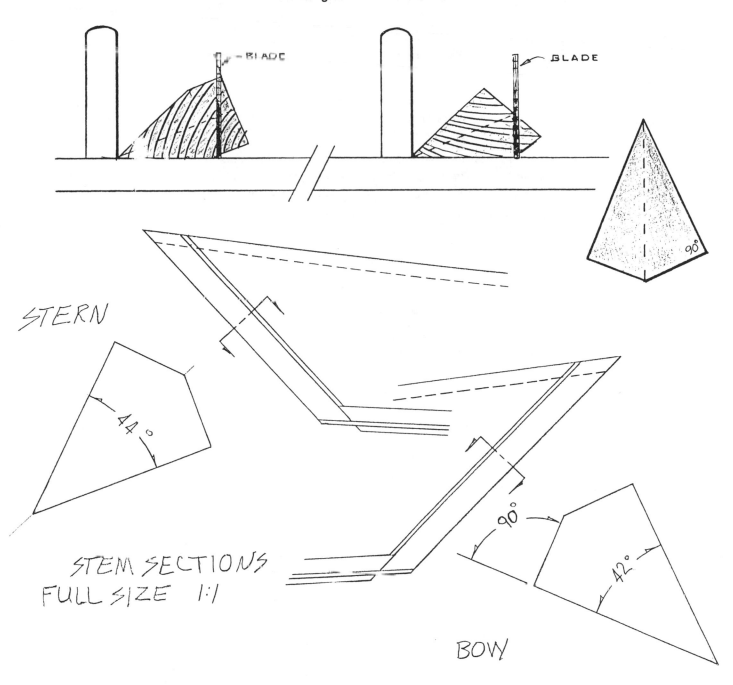

STERN

STEM SECTIONS
FULL SIZE 1:1

BOW

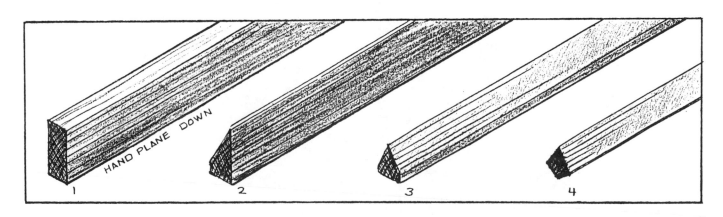

HAND PLANE DOWN

1   2   3   4

Section 5. Marking and Cutting the Gussets

The gussets reinforce the frame.

Using the full sized pattern, transfer the lines to a piece of 1/4" plywood. (Scrap from the 4 x 16 panel can be used.)

Using a hand saber saw, a scroll saw or a band saw, cut out the gussets. If you cut outside the line you can sand or plane to the line for a more precise fit. Mark the positions of the nail holes and drill them with a drill bit the size of the shaft of your ring nails. Do not drill holes in the corners where the notches for the chine logs go. (See Section 7).

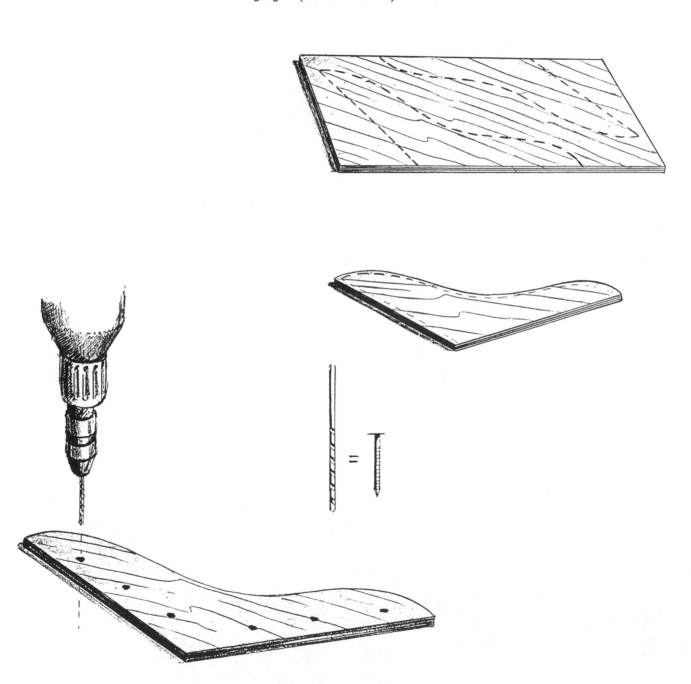

Section 8. Milling the Stock for the Frame, Gunwales and Chine Logs.

The dimensional lumber can now be cut on a table saw to the dimensions indicated on the plans and materials lists. Or you can substitute 1" x 2" stock (actually 3/4" x 1 1/2") from your lumber yard if you do not have access to a table saw.

Be sure to mark each piece with its part name to avoid confusion later. (See the materials list for the measurements for the various parts.)

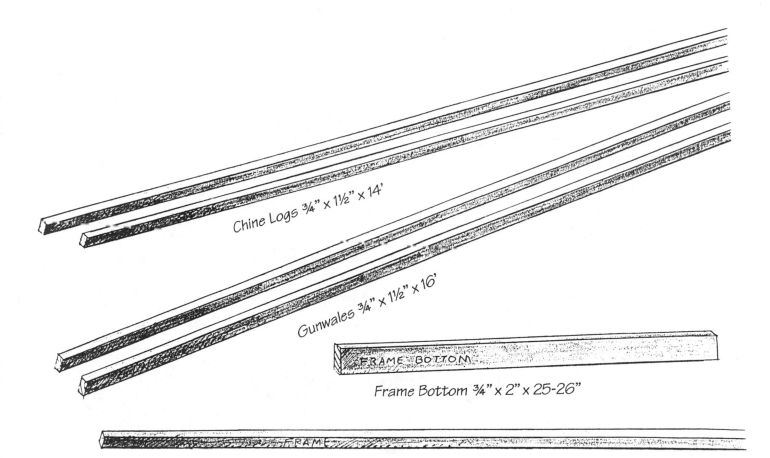

Chine Logs ¾" x 1½" x 14'

Gunwales ¾" x 1½" x 16'

FRAME BOTTOM

Frame Bottom ¾" x 2" x 25-26"

FRAME

Frames ¾" x 1½" x 5'

Section 7. Assembling the Frame

The frame is located just aft of the mid line of the boat, giving the boat its shape.

Using the pattern, mark the angles of the ends of the frame pieces and then use a hand or power saw to cut the frame members to the dimensions and angles as they appear on the pattern. Apply epoxy to the frame pieces and clamp them into position as shown. You will trim the frame sides to length and round them off after they are installed in the boat. Apply epoxy to the gussets and frame and glue and nail the gussets in place. Wipe off excess epoxy and set the frame aside to dry as soon as you are finished to prevent the epoxy from gluing the frame to the surface you are working on. (Note: You can use waxed paper on your work bench to prevent the epoxy from sticking.)

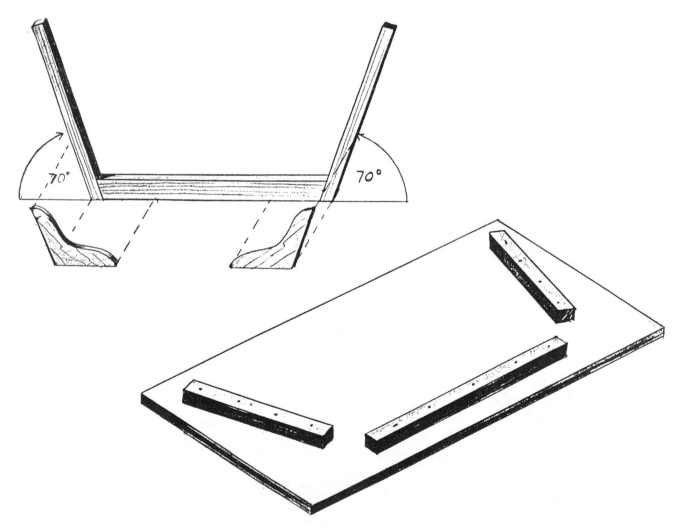

Note: If a number of boats are to be built, it may be wise to construct a jig as shown. This will enable quick and accurate positioning of frame pieces for gluing and nailing. If a jig is used, care must be taken to remove the frame and wipe off excess epoxy as soon as the frame is nailed.

Cutting the Chine Log Notches

At the bottom of each side of the frame you will need to use a hand saw or saber saw to cut the notches for the chine logs as shown on the plans. Lay a piece of your chine log stock on the frame as shown and mark the position of the notches, taking care to allow for the bevel that you will plane in the chine log after it is attached to the boat.

Cut out the notches.

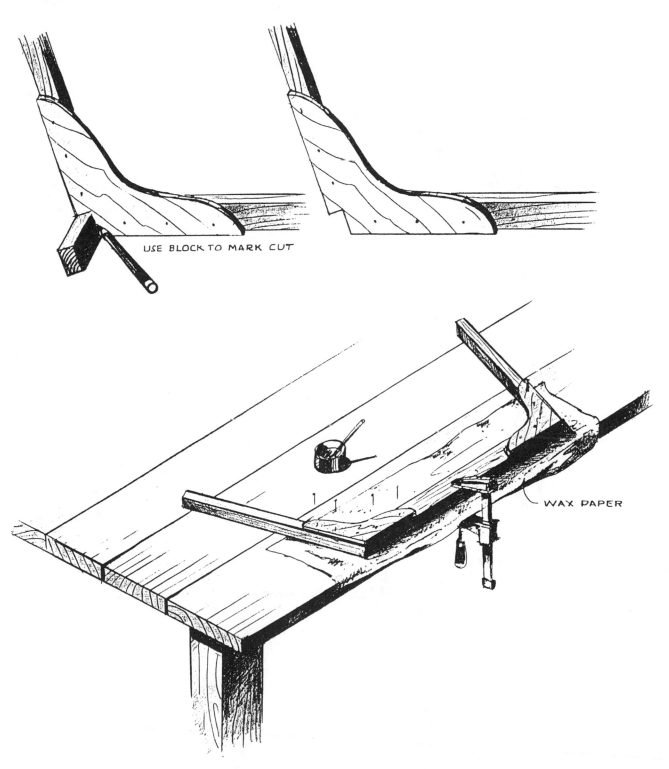

USE BLOCK TO MARK CUT

WAX PAPER

Section 8. Attaching the Stems

The stem pieces need to be epoxied and nailed to the bow and stern of one of the panels.
Lay the stem pieces on the appropriate ends and mark their positions with a pencil line. (Remember the bow and stern stem are slightly different so don't mix them up!)

MARK POSITION

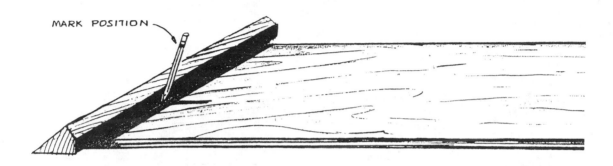

Clamp them in place and turn the panel over so you can drive in two or three 1" drywall screws, securing the stems to the panel. This is a dry run.

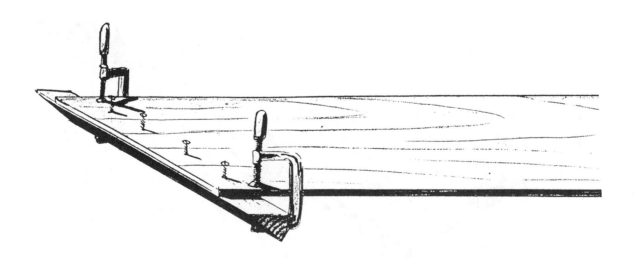

Take the drywall screws out and apply plenty of epoxy to the surfaces to be glued. Use the drywall screws to join the pieces together, again. Turn the panel over and nail the panel and stem together with 7/8" bronze ring nails at 2" intervals. Repeat at the other end.

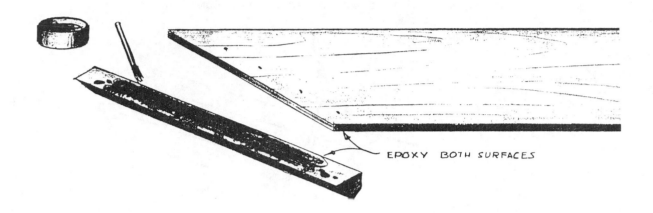

EPOXY BOTH SURFACES

(**Note:** You can also use drywall screws at 2" intervals, eliminating the ring nails. After the epoxy sets, you can remove the screws and fill the holes. Or, you can use 3/4" #8 bronze screws and leave them in.)

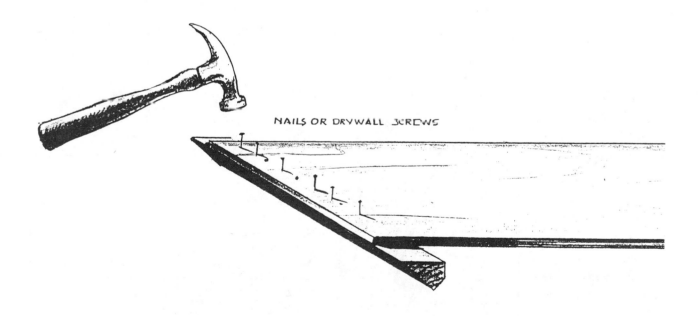

NAILS OR DRYWALL SCREWS

Section 9. Attaching the Frame

The frame will be screwed and epoxied in place on the side panels, one side at a time. Use 3/4" #8 bronze screws for this purpose and sink them just below the surface.

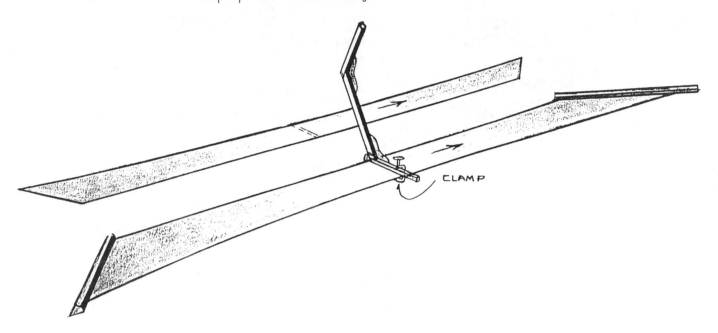

Lay the panels down with the inside facing up. Position the frame on one panel on the frame lines you marked earlier. Be sure the gusset side of the frame is facing forward. Use a straight edge as shown to match the bottom edge of the frame to the bottom edge of the inside of the panel. Mark this position exactly and clamp the frame in place.

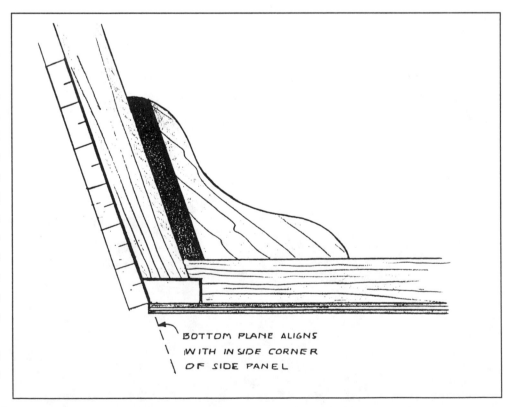

BOTTOM PLANE ALIGNS WITH INSIDE CORNER OF SIDE PANEL

Set the panel up so you can drill pilot holes and drive in four bronze screws.
Remove the screws and repeat the process on the other side.

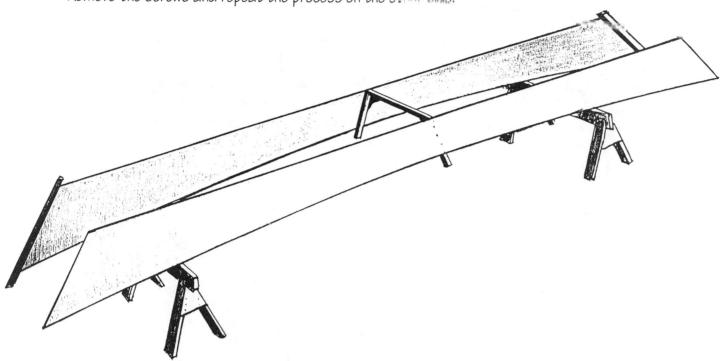

Remove the screws from the second side, apply epoxy to each surface and drive the screws back in again, taking care to match the holes exactly.

Set the panels up on saw bucks and epoxy and screw the frame to the remaining panel.

Wipe off any excess epoxy.

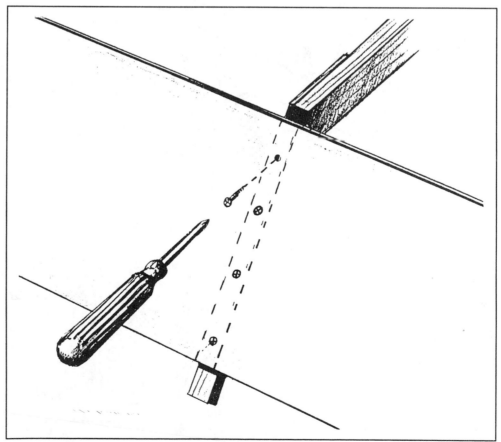

Section 10. Closing in the Side Panels

This is one of the most exciting parts of the process because your boat will finally take shape during this step.

Carefully position the bow end of the side panels so they match perfectly and drive in three drywall screws. "Eyeball" the results to be sure the sheer and bottom ends match and that the forward edges come together right at the stem piece. In other words, be sure your bow is symmetrical.

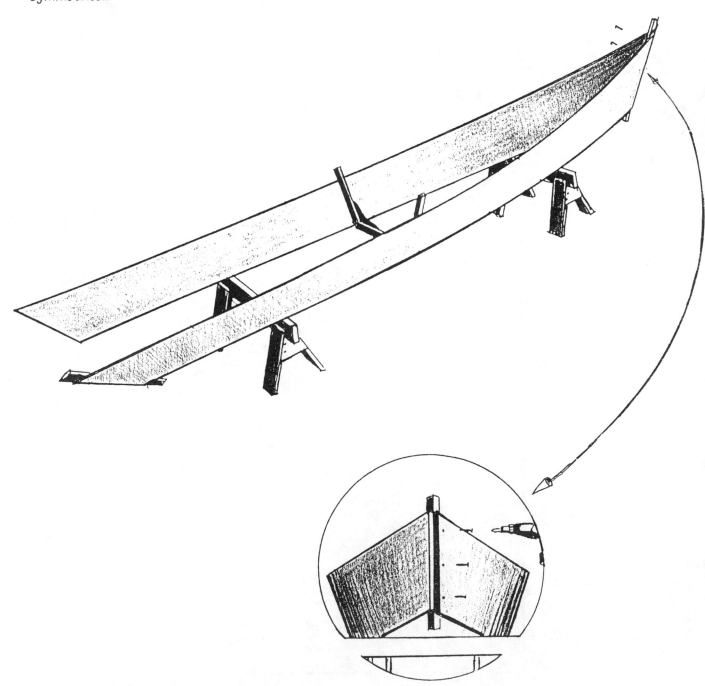

Repeat the process at the stern end.

Return to the bow and remove the drywall screws and apply epoxy to the match surfaces. Reassemble the bow.

Quickly, repeat the process at the stern end.

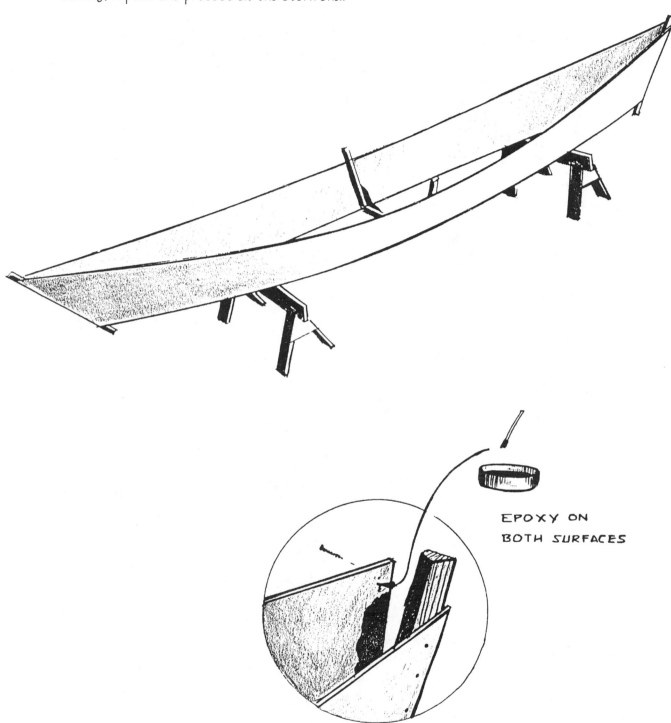

EPOXY ON
BOTH SURFACES

As soon as the stern is reassembled, turn the boat upside-down and nail in the ring nails as you did when you attached the stems to the other sides. Do this at both ends before the epoxy begins to "kick off".

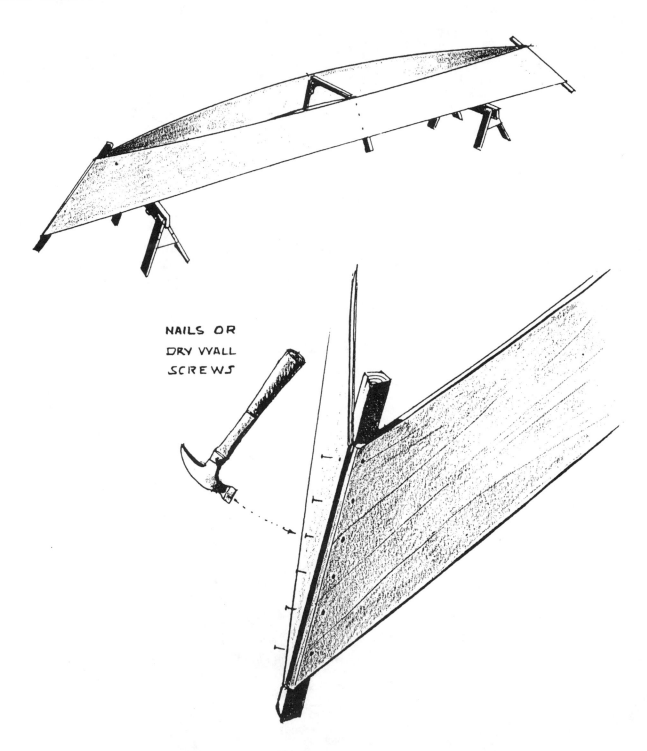

NAILS OR
DRY WALL
SCREWS

Take a few minutes to sit in your chair and admire what you've accomplished!

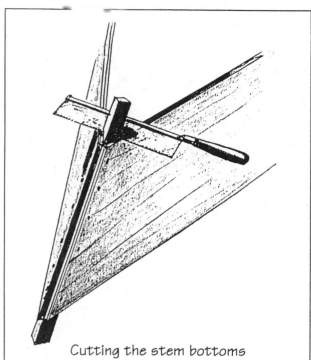

Cutting the stem bottoms

Cutting the stem bottoms

Once the epoxy cures you can cut the stems flush with the bottom edge of the canoe sides. This will complete Section 10.

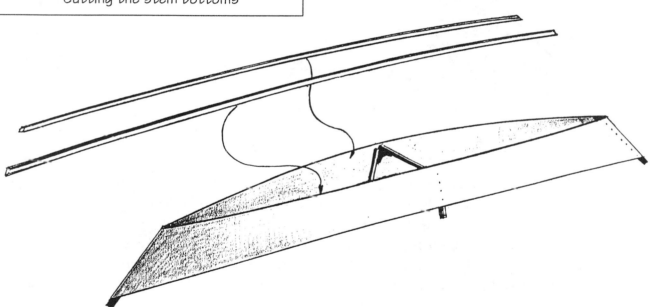

Section 11. Cutting, Installing and Planing the Chine Logs

The chine log is the structural member that the side and bottom panels are joined to. This joint needs to fit tightly so that there are no gaps where water might enter and hold moisture that over time will cause rot. This step is probably the most demanding and should not be hurried.

The chine logs are cut out of the 14' pieces of 3/4" x 1 1/2" stock. (Or the 1" x 2" stock you bought at the lumberyard so you wouldn't have to find the table saw.)

All of the following processes are done while the boat is upside down.

With a sliding t-bevel, take the angle of the bow, where the stem meets the bottom of the side panel on the inside of the canoe. Layout this angle on one end of each of the chine logs. Use a handsaw and a guide to cut this angle on one end of one of the chine logs, which will be the bow ends. With the bow angles cut, go to the stern and repeat the process, measuring and cutting. Don't worry that the chine logs are too long.

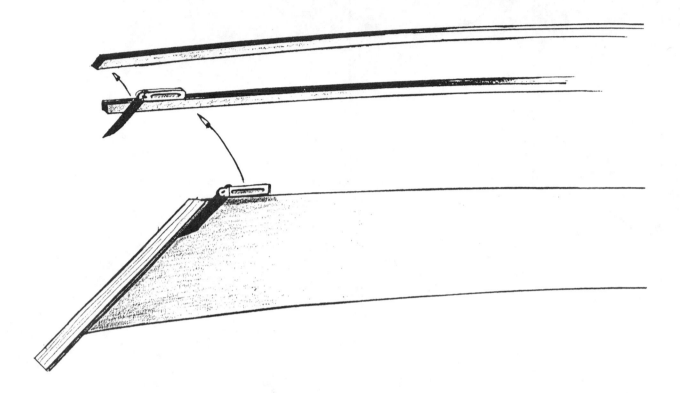

This is the step where you will determine the exact length of each chine log. With the chine log in the frame notch, slide the bow end up against the stem and clamp in place. (Note that the log rises above the side panel at the frame at the frame about a ¼". This height is proper and you should maintain it the entire length of the canoe. When you plane the log flat you will plane to the inside edge which will give you a flat surface on which the bottom will fit.)

With the bow end of the log in place make a pencil line across the chine log at the forward face of the frame (the bow end). This reference is important. Remove the log and slide the stern end in and repeat the process. The reference line across the chine will be marked once again at the forward face of the frame.

The distance between the two lines you marked is the exact length you have to cut off to get the chine log to fit.

Mark the distance at one end of the chine log and cut it off, being sure to retain the proper angle of the end you decided to cut off.

Insert the chine log and try it out. If it is still too long, trim it to fit. If, for some reason, it is too short you can insert a filler piece when you epoxy the chine log in place. Try to avoid that mistake on the other side.

Repeat the process on the other side.

When both sides fit, draw a line along the chine logs on the inside of the panels. This will mark the outline of the chine logs so you can apply epoxy in the right place.

Remove the chine logs and apply epoxy to one set of matching surfaces, reinstall the chine log and clamp in place. Nail ring nails every 2" along the chine log, from the outside. (Or you can use 3/4" drywall screws every 2" until the epoxy sets. When the epoxy is set you will then back the drywall screws out and fill the holes.)

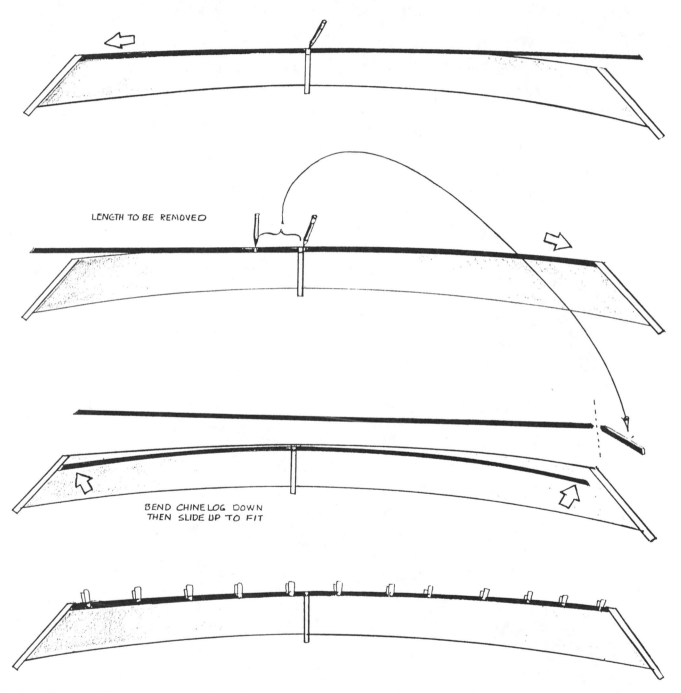

LENGTH TO BE REMOVED

BEND CHINE LOG DOWN
THEN SLIDE UP TO FIT

Repeat the process on the other side, being careful to line the second chine log up with the first, at each end. "Eyeball" it to be sure it looks okay.

Planing the Chine Logs

Planing is one of the most satisfying woodworking processes. If you are not an experienced planer, practice on pieces of scrap until you get the hang of it. If you have problems setting the plane or getting the hang of it, get some help so you can really enjoy this part of the process.

After the epoxy sets, you can plane the chine logs so you have a flat surface on which to nail the bottom.

Using a block plane, gradually flatten each chine log so a straight edge, when laid across the chine logs, will show a flat surface. It is best to plane a few strokes on each side, checking often with the straight edge, to avoid error.

To avoid tearing out when planning the ends, always plane toward the center of the boat. And be sure your block plane is sharp and properly adjusted. To keep the boat from jumping around when you plane, you may want to hang a sand bag over the frame. This added weight will make the boat much more stable and make planning much more enjoyable.

When you are finished, check the edges one more time.

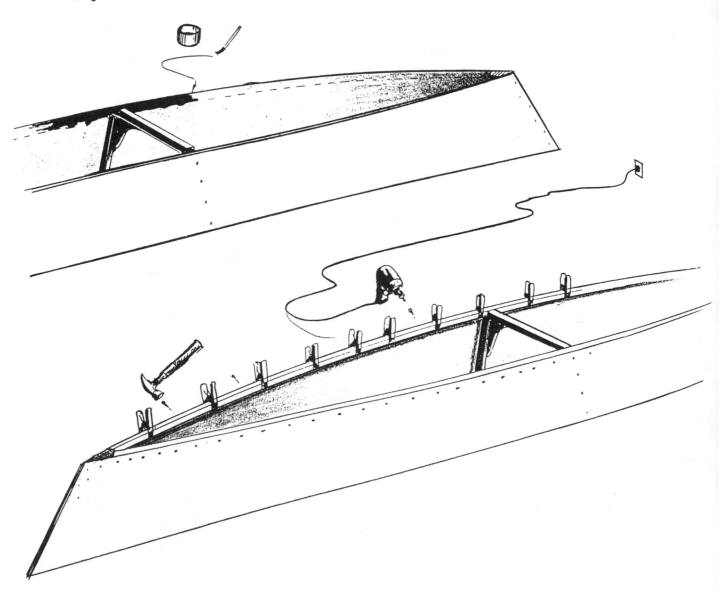

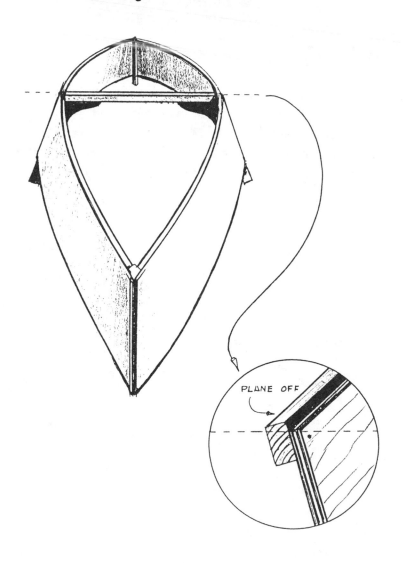

PLANE OFF

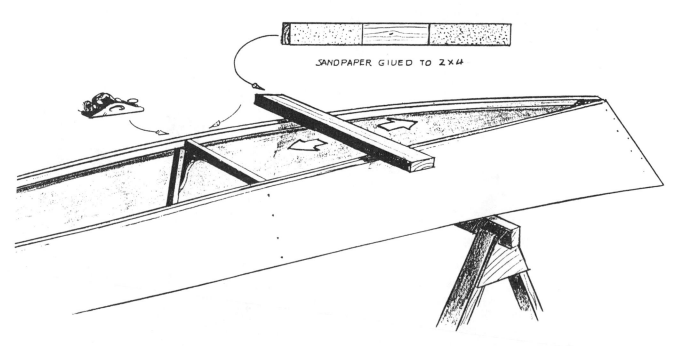

SANDPAPER GLUED TO 2 X 4

Section 12. Cutting and Installing the Gunwales

By attaching the gunwales now, you will strengthen the boat's sheer so when you nail the bottom on in the next step you won't risk shattering the plywood.

Turn the boat right-side up and clamp one of the gunwale pieces along one side. The top of the gunwale should come up to the sheer line you drew when you marked out the panels. Pre-drill holes from the inside and drive in 3/4" #8 bronze screws about every 3 inches along the length of the boat.

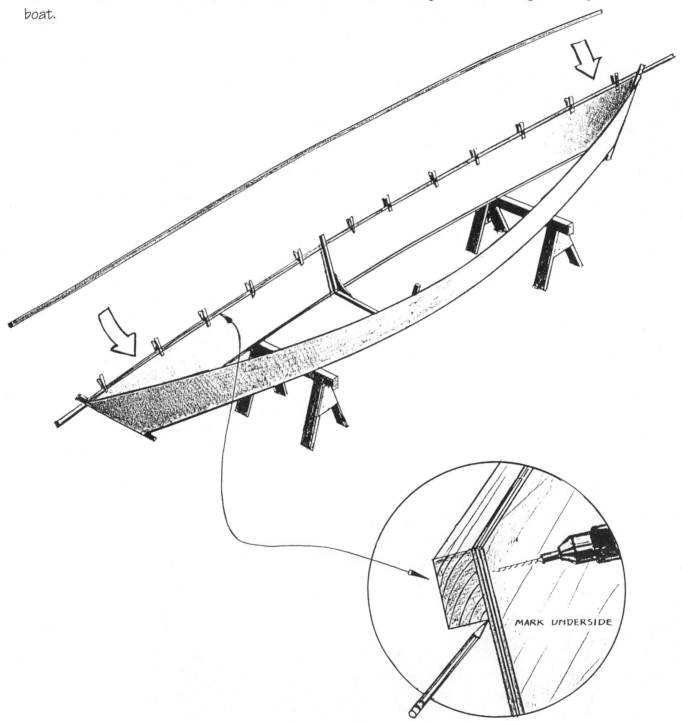

MARK UNDERSIDE

Draw a line along the bottom of the gunwale to mark the glue line and remove the gunwale. Apply epoxy to the matching surfaces and re-attach the gunwale.

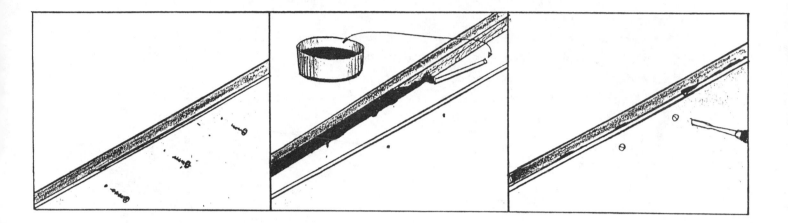

Turn the boat over and carefully lay a hand saw along the stem and trim off the part of gunwale that protrudes at each end.

Repeat the process for the other side.

Wipe off the excess epoxy.

Section 13. Cutting and Attaching the Bottom

Turn the boat upside down. Lay the bottom panel on the boat and line it up so the frame lines on the sides and on the bottom match up. Check to see that the frame lines on the bottom really are over the frame. This is important because you will be using these lines to tell you where to nail the bottom into the frame.

Put some weight on each end of the bottom to hold it in place and draw lines on the outside and on the inside to mark the glue lines. While you are drawing, check to see if the bottom lays flat on the chine logs. If not, take it off and do some more planing.

Take the bottom off and use a saber saw or hand saw and cut off the excess, leaving about 1/4" to 1/2" outside the line.

Apply a generous coating of epoxy to the matching surfaces on the bottom, the frame cross member and chine logs, and lay the bottom back on. Be sure you line it up.

Put some weight on both ends and begin nailing with ring nails at the center, alternating sides as you work your way toward each end. It is best to only partially drive the first nails and check the bottom alignment one more time before driving them home and continuing. Drive nails about every 2 inches. Don't forget to nail the bottom to the cross member of the frame.

Wipe off the excess epoxy.

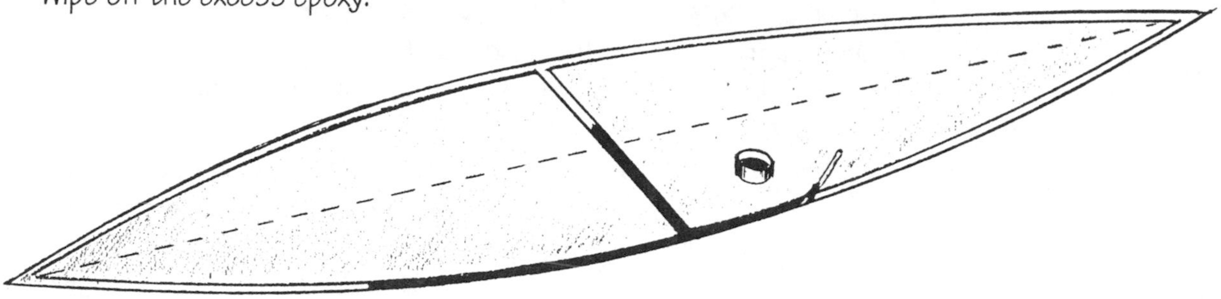

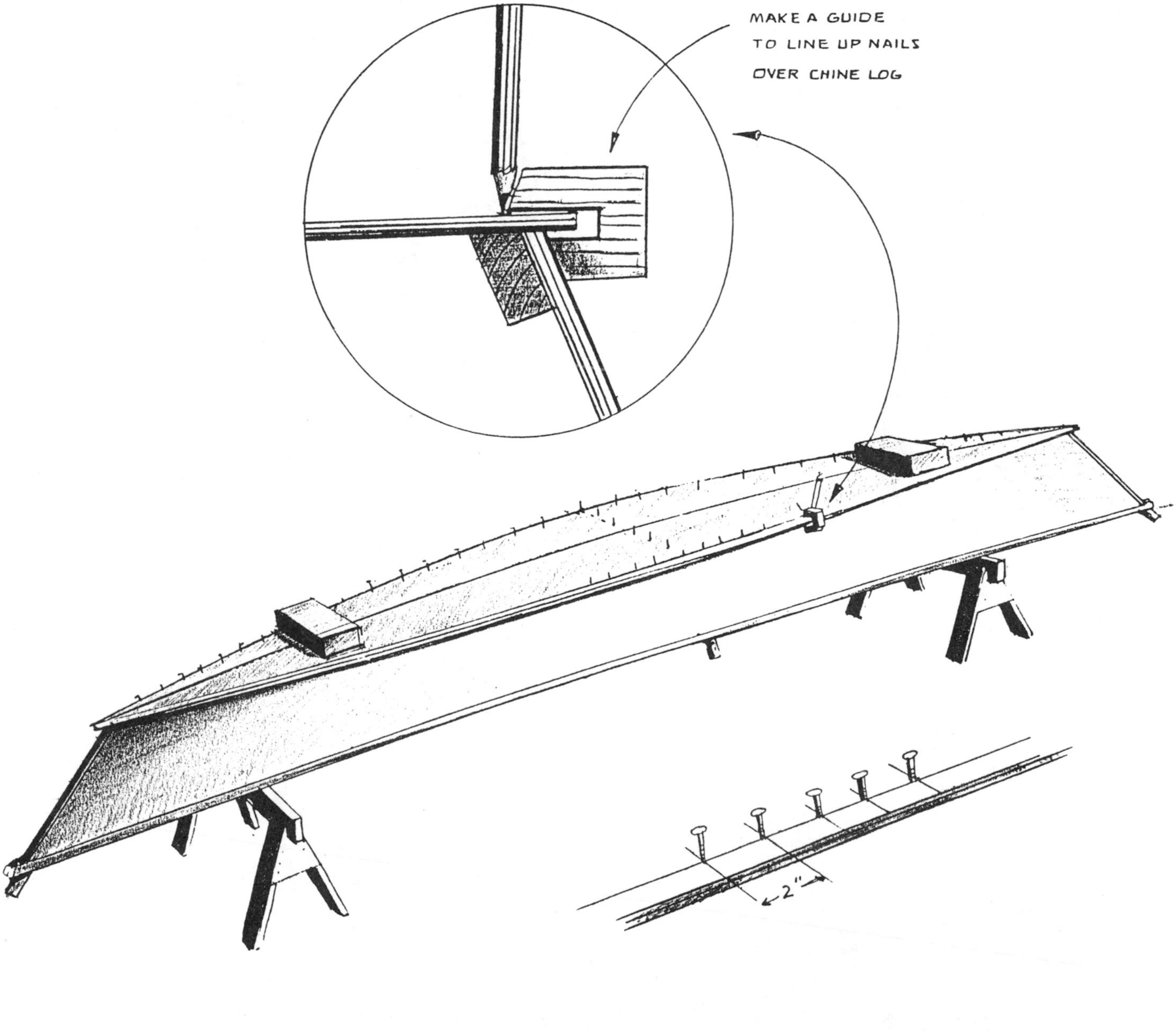

MAKE A GUIDE
TO LINE UP NAILS
OVER CHINE LOG

2"

Section 14. Trimming the Bottom and Sheer

Trimming the Bottom

After the epoxy sets, use a block plane to carefully trim off the overlap on the bottom. Take your time and be careful not to gouge the sides. If you have access to a router you can save time by trimming off with a flush trim bit and finishing with the block plane.

At this time you can also begin planing the stem ends, working down from the bottom toward the gunwales. Plane the stem ends flat.

After planing you can use a sanding block to get the chine line (bottom edge) and stem ends really clean. If you have access to power sanders this is the time to begin using them but be careful not to get carried away and gouge the plywood.

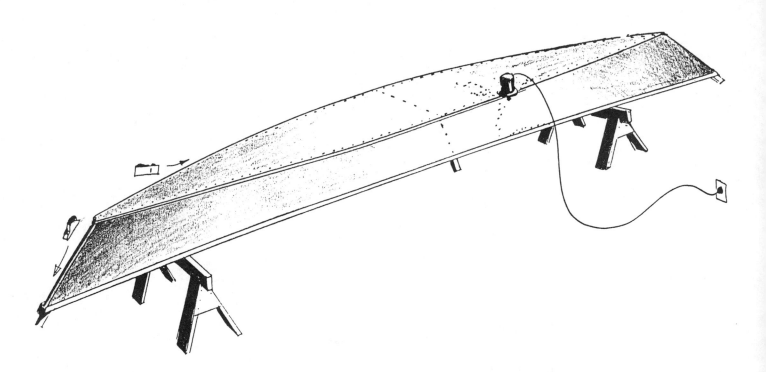

Trimming the Sheer

First cut off the tops of the stems. Lay a hand saw on a gunwale to the stem and use the gunwale as a guide, cutting forward until the stem is off. Do this on the opposite side to cut off a small sliver and you will end up with a peaked stem top - a nice detail. Repeat at the other end.

Now "eyeball" the sheer and plane the sheer smooth and true, using a block plane. If the grain cooperates you should work from the center toward the ends.

After the sheer is true, you should use your block plane and sanding block to round off the edges of the gunwales and the inside edge of the boat so the wood doesn't split off over time and so it is more comfortable to handle. (If you are going to add decks you should not round off the inside edge until the decks are installed.)

This would also be a good time to finish planing the tops of the stem ends at the ends of the gunwales and to sand the end grain of the gunwales.

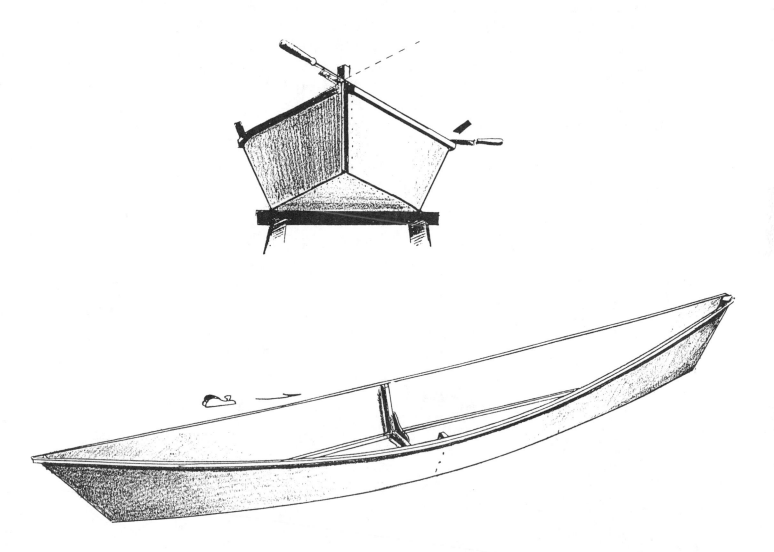

Section 15. Sanding and Finishing

Now it is time to finish off the boat.

Sanding, Filling and Taping

Use a dust mask when sanding. These dusts can be hazardous.

Begin by filling all of the holes and dings in the surface of the boat. You can use epoxy with a thickener or "Bondo", available at car parts stores. After filling, sand the filled areas and apply another coat, if necessary, sanding again until the filled area is fair.

After filling, sand the entire boat, either by hand or with a power sander, using a fairly coarse sand paper such as #50 and moving up to at least #150. Be careful to sand only with the grain, never across the grain.

At this point you have the option to apply fiberglass tape along the bottom seams. The advantage in doing this is a more damage resistant chine. If you choose this option, use 3" tape and carefully cut it to fit the seams, mitering at the ends where the tape might overlap. Lay down a coat of epoxy along the seams and bed the tape in the epoxy. Immediately apply more epoxy over the tape, smoothing it as you do. After the epoxy kicks off you can begin the process of sanding and applying more epoxy until the edge is smooth. You will probably have to use thickened epoxy or "Bondo" to fair off the entire area. Be sure to read the directions on the epoxy to learn how to re-coat. Some epoxies need sanding or even washing down with solvent before recoating. Take your time, if you choose this option, so you get a clean surface when you are finished.

Another option is to simply saturate all of the edges of the plywood with epoxy and sand them after the epoxy has set. This prevents water soaking of the plywood and strengthens the edges without the trouble of applying fiberglass tape.

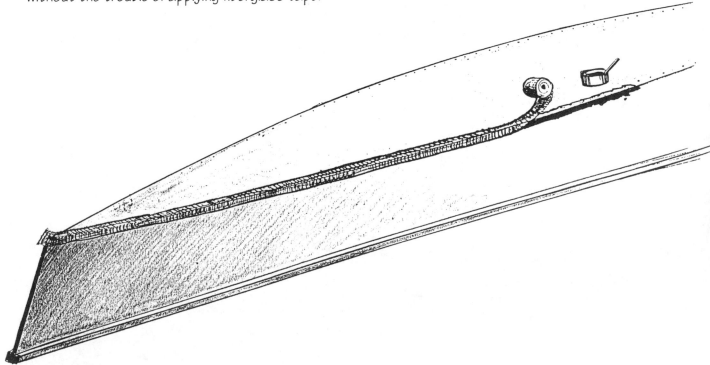

Painting and Varnishing

At this point you have many options. You can paint the entire boat with house paint or you can use yacht finishes and varnish. It really depends on how much time you want to spend and how you will use the boat. We have found that good primers and enamels and varnished gunwales produce a handsome boat without great cost or effort.

To begin, mask off your side panels and apply several coats of varnish to the gunwales, lightly sanding between coats. The new 3M artificial steel wool pads work great here.

Then, cover your gunwales with masking tape and apply primer inside and then on the outside of the boat. We have found that a sandable marine primer, while more expensive, hardens up more quickly and allows for a final sanding to get rid of little nicks and scratches. But you can also use oil based house primer.

After priming, lightly sand the surface and wipe off the dust.

For the final coat (s) you can use a semi-gloss marine enamel or a good quality latex house paint. Depending on the paint, you may need several coats and, if you use latex paint, allow several weeks before subjecting the boat to hard use so the paint can harden up.

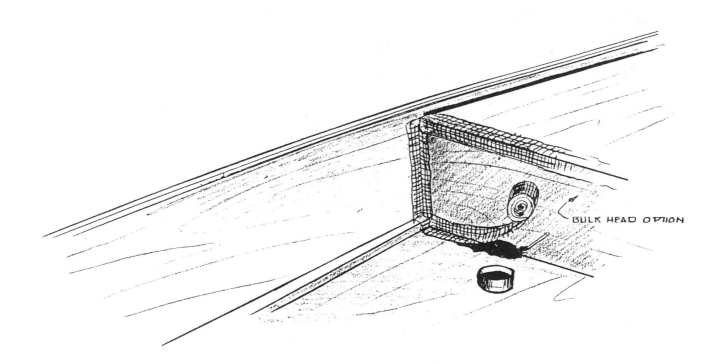

BULK HEAD OPTION

Section 16. Deck Options

The Six-Hour Canoe can be built with or without decks. Building without decks results in a lightweight boat and many like its simple lines. Building with deck can offer flotation and storage options but does so at an increase in weight.

The illustrations show several deck options and each can be built with or without bulkheads and flotation.

To add decks you will need to make cardboard templates and fit them accurately before cutting the actual plywood. Install bulkheads first and paint or coat the interior surfaces with epoxy before attaching the decks. You may also want to drill a 1" drainage/ventilation hole in the bottom of each bulkhead to discourage mildew and rot.

When installing bulkheads you can use fiberglass tape and thickened epoxy on the inside for a strong joint. Decks need to be set on cleats that have been fastened to the side panels and bulkheads.

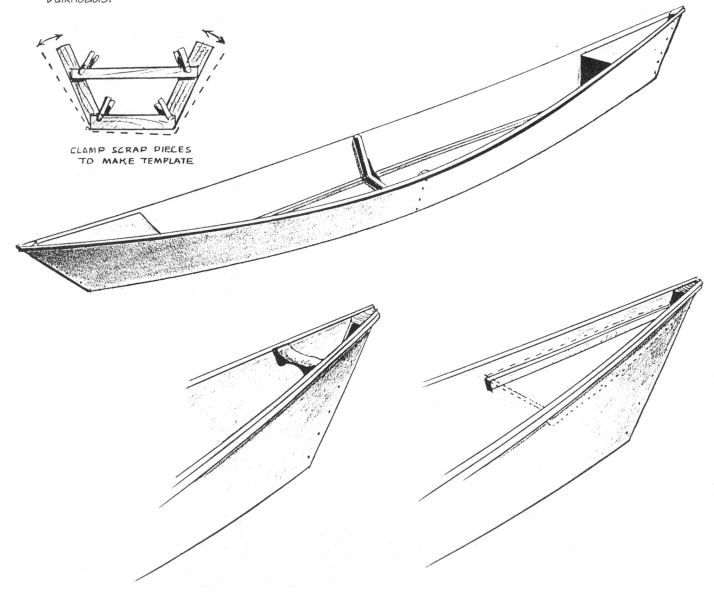

CLAMP SCRAP PIECES
TO MAKE TEMPLATE

Section 17. Flotation Options

Adding flotation increases the margin of safety and leads to greater peace of mind. This is particularly true in a small boat that will be used by kids. Built of wood, the canoe will float when tipped but, with flotation, it is easier to right and bail out after a spill.

At the very least, life jackets must always be worn and it is wise to have a class IV boat cushion aboard for each occupant. There are several other options, though.

The first is to secure air bags, used in kayaks, to each end of the boat. These bags can be obtained at dealers who sell kayaks and at many outdoor outfitters such as L. L. Bean. Secure them with bungee cords by attaching a series of screw eyes or cleats secured to the chine logs.

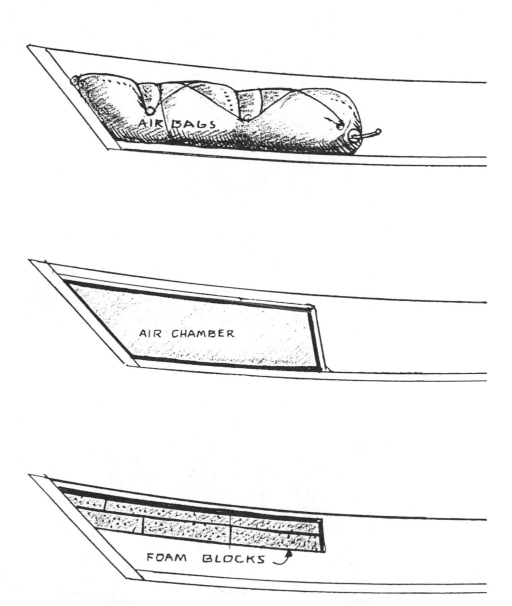

The advantage of air bags is that you don't need decks or bulkheads and have the option to take them out when carrying the boat. The disadvantage is that they are not cheap.

The other option is to install foam flotation under decks at either end. Remember that displacing one cubic foot will give you about 62 pounds of flotation. You can buy two part expandable foam and foam the flotation in place if you install bulkheads and decks. The advantage to such flotation is that it is always there. The disadvantage is that it adds weight to the boat.

Section 18. Seating Options

The Six-Hour Canoe is designed to be paddled, kayak style, from the center of the boat. If two kids are using the boat, it can be propelled, at each end, with canoe paddles.

For the center position the illustrations show several options. All show the seat low in the boat to keep the center of gravity down for maximum stability. Higher seats will make the canoe very unstable. In any case you should install some sort of back rest to reduce fatigue. And, try to build the lightest seat you can. I know one person who installed a cut-off high backed chair in his boat!

Section 19. Keels

For most applications a keel greatly increases the directional stability of the boat. We have found that a keel, made of 3/4" stock, running the length of the boat, works very well. Since keels take a lot of abuse, it is best to attach the keel at the very end of the building process. Bed the keel in marine bedding compound and screw it to the bottom, from the inside, so it can be replaced easily. Use 3/4" bronze screws and paint the keel.

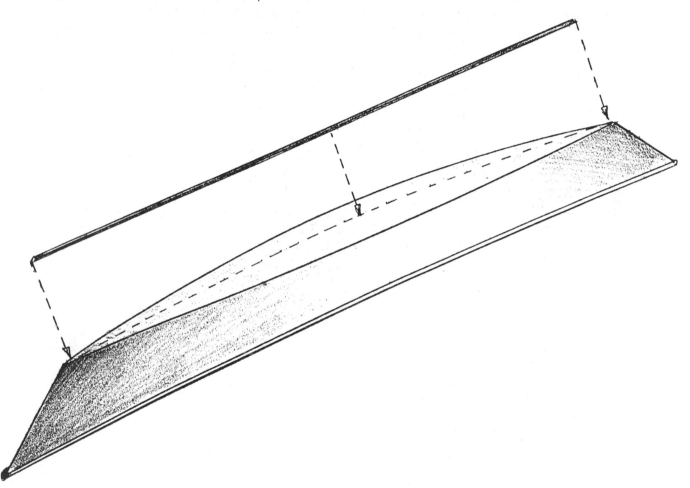

Section 20. Final Thoughts

   Congratulations! Your boat is finished and you can sit back in the boat builder's chair and relish the results. Before you launch, however, lets review some important points.

❑ The boat is intended for one adult or two kids - no more than 250 lbs. Don't overload it.

❑ It is also intended for quiet waters - lakes, pond, lazy rivers. Rough or fast waters can swamp the boat or drive it against rocks where the light-weight hull can easily be holed.

❑ Always use approved life jackets when operating the boat.

❑ Keep children under supervision when they are aboard.

❑ When using the boat for the first time, give yourself an opportunity to get to know its capabilities. Tip it over in shallow water to see how it floats and what it takes to right it.

❑ If you are an inexperienced boater, you may want to take a canoe instruction or water safety course to increase your margin of safety.

PART II

PADDLING TECHNIQUE AND SAFETY

by Mike O'Brien

Paddling the Six-Hour Canoe

The Six-Hour Canoe is a solo boat for careful paddlers and swimmers to use in warm and shallow waters. It is not intended for, and should not be used in, rough and cold water. U.S. Coast Guard-approved PFDs (personal flotation devices, i.e., life jackets) should be worn at all times, and the canoe should be fitted with positive-buoyancy flotation (inflated bags or closed-cell foam blocks). Paddlers should follow safety advice found in standard references, such as: **Canoeing and Kayaking** (American Red Cross, 1981), **Sports Illustrated Canoeing** (Time, Inc., 1981), and **Canoeing and Kayaking Instruction Manual** (American Canoe Association, 1987).

Underway, this canoe ought to be trimmed down slightly by the stern. Paddlers of normal mass will achieve this desirable state of affairs simply by sitting on a cushion placed on the bottom of the boat directly abaft the 'midship frame. (The lower a paddler sits, the better for stability and comfort. Should you decide to mount a permanent seat in the canoe, keep it

extremely low.) If additional cargo is brought aboard, keep it low, and adjust its position so that the heel of the canoe's stem barely kisses the water. Take care not to overload this, or any other, canoe. Trimmed in this way, the little plywood boat wants to go in a straight line, but not to the point of being stubborn about it.

As for paddling technique, experience is a far better teacher than words can ever be, but if you'll permit me a few random thoughts: Your mother told you first, and now I'll say it — sit up straight! When paddling use only the lower portion of the backrest for support (lean way back for resting). Hold the paddle away from your body, and twist your torso as you stroke, so as to use the big all-day muscles in your back. With each stroke, bury the working paddle-blade in the water just enough to completely submerge it — then apply the power. Don't go too deep. Strive for a fluid and gentle motion; speed will come naturally.

Early on, you must come to terms with the question posed to all users of double-bladed paddles: To feather or not to feather? Feathered paddles have their blades set at

angles (usually 90°) to each other. Unfeathered (that is, 0° feather) paddles have their blades secured in the same plane. Feathered paddles enjoy some advantage going to windward in a breeze, and they permit the relatively wide blades favored by racers and whitewater paddlers to clear the water's surface more easily. But they tend to be noisier and wetter than unfeathered paddles, and they can prove less secure with the wind on the beam. As may be, the idea held by some observers that paddlers who feather their blades are better than those who don't seems to be of contemporary origin, and it ignores the exploits of countless generations of Inuit paddlers who relied upon narrow unfeathered blades.

After choosing a favorite angle of feather, try to stay with it. Bracing (placing a paddle blade flat on the water to provide stability) becomes instinctive. Altering feather angles too often might result in your throwing out a brace with a blade perpendicular, rather than parallel, with the water's surface. And that can ruin your whole day.

Safety

Paddling is both a complex and a natural motion. Study the basics, but try not to think too hard while you're practicing. Let your body do the work, you'll know when everything feels right. David Seidman, in his superb book The *Essential Sea Kayaker* (Ragged Mountain Press, 1992), summarized some fundamental points of double-bladed paddling. They are paraphrased below, and they are well worth cataloging somewhere in the back of your mind:

- Keep the power blade fully immersed and perpendicular to the water's surface.
- Center your grip on the shaft, and keep it fairly loose.
- Sit upright with your head steady.
- Hold the paddle shaft away from your chest, and keep your elbows slightly bent.
- Place the blade as far ahead as possible at the beginning of the stroke, without bending forward at your waist — twist, don't lunge.
- Put the blade into the water cleanly with little splash.
- Use the palm of the upper hand to push, guided by slightly opened fingers.
- Maintain as shallow a shaft angle as is practical.
- Get the majority of your power from your torso, not your arms.
- Twist your torso and rotate your shoulders to pull one arm back while driving the other arm forward.
- Apply maximum power in mid-stroke, usually as the power-blade is passing your knees.
- Slice the blade up and cleanly out of the water as it passes your hip. (Avoid taking strokes that are too long.)
- Don't apply unnecessary force.

PART III

COMMUNITY BOAT BUILDING

Frankie and his sister had not seen each other in almost a year - a difficult year in which Lee Ann moved out of the house.

Sam's dad died when he was three. A bright eighth grader, he had been doing okay in school, but lately he was cutting classes and getting into fights.

More about these kids later, but first, what's urban boat building?

Four or five years ago we began to hear about programs that used boat building to build self-esteem in kids who were disadvantaged or who had suffered some kind of emotional trauma. Other programs used boat building to teach, in a soft way, hard concepts in math, science and writing. It seemed promising.

At the college we were building tortured plywood kayaks in the introductory classes. These classes were intended for students who had no prior boat building or woodworking experience and the objective of the course was to introduce them to craftsmanship and design in a hands-on experience.

What we were observing, however, went much deeper than the course objectives. The students were encountering very tough and unfamiliar problems and when they succeeded, they were incredibly proud of what they had done. It didn't matter what age they were, whether they were male or female or what their background was - they were proud when they finished their boats.

Buffalo State College is proud of its urban mission. Surrounded by city neighborhoods, affluent to the east of campus and mixed working class and disadvantaged in other directions, it has a special opportunity to work with school and community leaders to address the problems found in any metropolitan area.

The Buffalo Public Schools were among the first in the nation to develop the magnet school concept and there are many fine schools in the area surrounding the campus. But these schools draw from neighborhoods where unemployment is high, alcohol and drug use have exploded and their problems affect what goes on in the classroom. In short, we are sitting in the middle of an opportunity.

The opportunity began to present itself when several of us were in a meeting on funding possibilities for our program when somebody mentioned that we should meet Joe Murray. Joe was the man who developed the magnet school concept in Buffalo, and he had just retired from the public schools and was working at the college. We were told that Joe would have ideas about ways in which we could gain entry into the school to work with kids.

Joe did have ideas - it was easy to see why he was held in such high esteem by his colleagues in education. In fact, within a short time, Joe assembled a group of junior high technology teachers and obtained funding so we could offer them a course in kayak building in evening sessions. In addition to the building experience, we all hoped some ideas would come out of the experience that would point to future directions.

About six teachers participated and one of them, Chuck Knier, really took hold. Skeptical at first about the ability of junior high school students to build kayaks, Chuck's enthusiasm got the best of him and he was soon making plans to build a kayak at his school. Even more interesting about Chuck's school is that it is a Native American Magnet School which included grades K-8.

Buffalo is surrounded by Native American reservations and has a fairly high native population in the city. Many of the native people are economically distressed and many of their children opt to attend the Native American Magnet School #19 which is located only about a mile from our campus. It's an interesting school where the native culture is celebrated and where there are special opportunities for native kids to excel.

Chuck talked to his principal, Dr. Lloyd Elm - himself a Native American - and with the help of special funding arranged by Joe Murray, introduced kayak building in his technology classes. In that first year, they worked together to build a kayak and seeds began to germinate.

But there was a problem. The kayak was so complex and tricky to build that progress was slow and attention could waver - something Chuck foresaw at the beginning. It was clear that we needed a new boat, one that could be built more quickly and that might even be built, not by a whole class, but by a small team of people.

The Six-Hour Canoe seemed to be the answer. At the college we had discovered that it was essential that each student build his or her own boat and our students had built over a hundred and fifty kayaks on that premise. But we, too, found the kayaks to be awfully demanding and hard to finish in a ninety hour semester. They were not cheap either. So the Six-Hour Canoe, first proposed by Mike O'Brien, appeared to be a good alternative.

We built several canoes over the summer and adapted the design to our needs and aesthetic. And, in the fall semester, we introduced it to our classes. After the kayaks it was a dream, easily built in a semester, allowing us to spend more time on other important issues such as the evolution of boat design and so on. Chuck was watching and soon followed suit in his program.

First, the canoe was used in regular classes as Chuck had used the kayak. But we knew there was potential for something more. After a year of experimentation and consulting we proposed that the college and native School try "team boat building".

TEAM BOAT BUILDING

Dr. Elm had mentioned, at a meeting, that it would be useful if we could bring the native kids to our campus. College education had been out of reach for most of their parents and he wanted the kids to begin to see it as a possibility for themselves. With the success of the Six-Hour Canoe in Chuck Knier's classes and the enthusiasm it generated, we began to come up with an idea.

In the spring of 1993, we invited the Native American Magnet School to select up to ten students and their families to participate in a weekend boat building program. Again, with funding arranged by Joe Murray and the Rotary Club, we had obtained the materials so we could offer a boat to each family, at no cost. We would supply the shop and the mentors, and the Native School would provide Chuck Knier and the students and their families.

The idea was to involve our students and friends of the program, all of who had built Six-Hour Canoes, to serve as mentors. Team boat building offered the opportunity to build boats and relationships so we selected our mentors carefully. Many were education majors, several were non-traditional students, several were boat building majors, but all shared an enthusiasm for the process and an ability to relate to people. And all promised to stick with it from beginning to end.

It was also important to get results quickly, to maintain a high level of interest, so we planned the experience around a four day schedule - a Saturday and Sunday and two subsequent Saturdays. And, we hoped to get the hulls finished in the first weekend. To accomplish this rigorous schedule we decided to pre-cut the panels, stems and frame. So each team began with a "kit" of pre-cut pieces.

At 8:00 a.m. on the first Saturday the families began to arrive and continued to arrive over the next several hours. Suspicious of our culture's motives, after a century of betrayal, the Native American families were very quiet, at first. After coffee and donuts, the teams got to work and the mentors took over.

Frankie, who came with his mother, held back at first. Peter, his mentor, knew that it was important for Frankie and his mother to build the boat, so he showed them how and urged them to do it. Gradually, by the end of the morning, both were intently assembling parts and panels and Peter was only interceding when absolutely necessary.

Around noon, Frankie's sister showed up. She had built a canoe the year before and then had gone onto high school. As an "expert" she was a real help and Frankie's mother told us how pleased she was at these turn of events.

By late morning the first team had glued on its stems and frame and had brought the boat up - it looked like a boat. We called a halt and presented a "trophy", an inflated rubber glove, to that team as an acknowledgment of their accomplishment. Joe took the "trophy" home that night.

Sam had come with his uncle, a young man who was shepherding his nephews, all of whom had lost their fathers. We assigned John, an attorney, as their mentor and the team worked smoothly from the beginning. Sam's uncle was a caring man who stuck with it through the whole process and, when Native People were asked to carry the torch for the World University Games, which were held in Buffalo that summer, Sam and his uncle took the torch in their canoe and paraded with it through Buffalo harbor. It was a proud moment for the both of them.

By the end of the first day all of the canoes were up, chine logs were in and everybody went home tired but feeling pretty good.

The second day, the families planed the chine logs, fitted and trimmed the bottoms and attached the gunwales. When all the boats had reached that point we had a barbecue to celebrate. The families and their mentors turned their boats upside down and used them for picnic tables. Suspicions over, the teams were working smoothly and everybody felt good about what they had accomplished.

The next Saturday the families returned to sand and prime their boats. And, on the following Saturday they returned to apply the finish coats of paint. We told them they could come back during the week, after their paint was dry, to add details. Several families added interesting designs to the bows of their boats.

The launching was a gala affair. Next to campus is the site of the 1901 Columbian Exposition and the casino and lake, part of a park system designed by Frederick Law Olmstead, remain. With the cooperation of the Native American Community and the casino operator, native dancers and craftspeople participated in a

Native American celebration and the launching was part of the program. All of the families, many friends and the mentors showed up. There were over two hundred people in attendance.

Frankie's family was there to watch him take his boat out on the maiden voyage. By far the largest kid in the group, Frankie was not very confident and his entire boat shook as he clung to the edge of the dock. With a glance toward his mother, who nodded approval, we shoved him off, fully expecting him to capsize. After a few tentative strokes with the double paddle he found his sea legs and was soon out there with the rest.

We talked about the launch day and safety. Chuck felt it important for the kids to experience their boats with minimal interference. We had equipped each builder with his own life jacket and laid down a few ground rules and the lake was small and sheltered. So, we put a few safety boats in the waters, manned by experienced boatmen, and left the kids alone. Within a few minutes they were at home in their boats and soon came in, proud, to show off their new found skills. Family members began to crowd the edge, waiting for a chance to take the boats out.

At the end of the day we took the boats back into storage and invited the families back for an evening session on boat handling and boating safety after which the boats would be theirs. Everybody attended the session.

WHAT WE LEARNED

Following is a series of observations and critiques on the entire experience:

Getting Started

❑ It is essential that you have an advocate in the school, club or whatever organization is involved in the process. In cases where we did not have such an advocate, a principal or a valued teacher, our program faltered.

❑ At the beginning, when we were training teachers, it helped to be able to offer in-service credit for recertification. This can be arranged through the Board of Education.

❑ Funding for our programs came from Boards of Education and from service organizations such as the Rotary Club.

❑ Mentors have been our students, friends and Rotary Club members. There are lots of latent and experienced boat builders out there who can be enticed to help.

❑ Offer one-day training sessions in which future mentors build a boat and receive a manual and set of plans. This is essential so the mentors feel confident in their ability to lead.

❑ Stipulate, in any training sessions, that the goal is to enable the student builders to do it themselves.

The Process

❑ To maintain interest, each participant should build his or her own boat. In community and school programs it is fairly easy to find sponsors for the boats at a cost of about $150 - $200 each.

❑ It is essential to keep the program moving. Try to set daily goals so you can see progress. Don't be afraid to challenge the participants as long as you have adequate support for them.

❑ Be completely organized so there is no standing around - a deadly condition. At the end of the day our participants were exhausted - but happy! There was no standing around.

❑ Seventh and eighth graders can put in productive eight hour days. In fact, we had to pull them away from their boats for lunch.

❑ Seventh and eighth graders can handle any power tools or process as long as a mentor is there to help. Parents watched approvingly, as their kids mastered routers, jig saws, etc.

❑ Don't be afraid to stop and celebrate accomplishments!

A Successful Program

Day One
(Saturday)

Preparation

❑ Pre-cut the panels and stems and assemble a frame for each boat. Mark the location of the frame on the inside of the side panels. Mark "bow" and "stern" on the side panels and appropriate stem pieces. Machine stock for chine logs and gunwales.

❑ Have a building station with a pair of saw horses, a hammer, a cordless drill and phillips bit, and a sharp block plane for each participant.

❑ Have epoxy, epoxy brushes, 6 spring clamps, 2 light bar clamps available for each boat.

❑ Have a general supply area with ring nails, 3/4" drywall screws, and sharp handsaws available.

Process

8:00 a.m. - 8:30 a.m.:

❑ *Team Meets (Coffee, milk, donuts, etc.)*

8:30 a.m.

❑ *Begin/Construction*

❑ Lay out the side panels and mark and attach the stems to one panel. Use epoxy and drywall screws.

❑ Mark the position of the frame on **both** panels inside and out.

❑ Cut out the chine notches in the frame.

❑ Attach the frame to both panels with drywall screws. Do not use epoxy yet.

❑ Join the bow sections together with drywall screws - no epoxy yet.

❑ Join the stern sections in the same manner.

❑ Take the pieces apart, apply epoxy and re-join in the same order.

12:00 p.m.-1:00 p.m.

❑ *Lunch*

1:00 p.m.

❑ Turn the boat upside down and install the chine logs one side at a time using drywall screws.

❑ Turn the boat right side up and install the gunwales.

4:00 p.m. - 5:00 p.m.

❑ *Finish for the Day*

DAY TWO
(Sunday)

Preparation

Same stations and tools as day one.

Process

12:00 p.m.

❑ **Continue**

❑ Remove all drywall screws.

❑ Cut off the protruding stem ends at the top and bottom.

❑ Turn the boat upside down and plane the chine logs.

❑ Attach the bottom using ring nails.

❑ Trim the gunwales and soften their edges with a plane.

❑ Trim the tops of the frame at the sheer, if needed.

❑ Plane the sheer line.

❑ Plane the stem ends.

5:00 p.m.

❑ **Finish for the Day**

5:30 p.m.

❑ **Barbecue and Picnic - Invite All Family Members!**

DAY THREE
(Saturday)

Preparation

❑ Have sandpaper and sanding blocks available in 80 and 120 grits.
❑ If possible, have a power block sander available for each station.
❑ Have a router with a flush trim bit available.
❑ A belt sander with 80 grit paper would also be useful.
❑ Have ample primer (about one quart) for each boat and several 3" throw away foam brushes.

Process

8:00 a.m. - 8:30 a.m.

❑ Coffee, milk, donuts, etc.

8:30 a.m.

❑ *Continue*

❑ Use router to trim the bottom of the boat.

❑ Use block planes and/or belt sander to finish trim chine edge.

❑ Drill holes for painters in bow and stern.

❑ Sand the boat.

12:00 p.m.- 1:00 p.m.   **Lunch**

1:00 p.m.

Remove all dust and prime the inside first, then the outside of the boat.

2:00 p.m. - 3:00 p.m.

❑ *Finish For The Day*

DAY FOUR
(Saturday)
etc.

Preparation

☐ One quart of paint for each boat and several 3" foam brushes

Process

9:00 a.m. - 9:30 a.m. Coffee, milk, donuts,

9:30 a.m. **Begin**

☐ Lightly sand the boat.

☐ Apply the finish coat of paint.

☐ Announce launch plans and festivities.

LAUNCH DAY

Preparation

❑ Select a quiet, sheltered place to launch. Avoid moving water or exposed and crowded launch sites.

❑ Arrange to have an experienced canoeist available to instruct new boat builders.

❑ Have several safety boats and experienced boaters in the water at launch time and whenever the new boats are in the water.

❑ Provide a certified life jacket for each participant and insure that they are worn.

Process

❑ Be sure a parent or guardian is present for each participant.

❑ Bring the boats to the water's edge.

❑ Instruct the participants, parents and guardians in safe boarding, from the beach and from a dock.

❑ Instruct in safe boating practices.

❑ Have participants put on their life jackets.

❑ Launch small boats in small groups - avoid chaos.

❑ Have an experienced double paddle kayaker or canoeist show the participants how to paddle, stop, turn and approach a beach and dock.

Note 1: It is important that participants understand that they are responsible for safe boating practices. Be sure they understand its load limit (250 lbs.) and application to sheltered waters.

Note 2: This four day schedule works! But you can adapt it to a different one by figuring on about 24 hours of building time from start to final coat of paint and breaking it up to fit your groups' needs. Remember - be organized and don't drag it on too long. Kids need to see results to stay involved. So do adults for that matter. ***Good Luck!***

Workshops are offered at the college, periodically, and the authors are available for on site workshops and consultation. For information or questions, contact:

Richard Butz, Director
Center for Watercraft Studies
State University College at Buffalo
1300 Elmwood Avenue
Buffalo, NY 14222
716-878-4823 (Shop)
716-649-8018 (Home)

APPENDICES

A. MATERIALS AND TOOLS LIST FOR THE SIX HOUR CANOE

MATERIALS:

Lumber

(See Butt Block Option in Appendix)

- ❑ 1 panel of 1/4" x 4' x 16" marine grade plywood (hull)
- ❑ 2 pcs. 3/4" x 1 1/2" x 14' knot free pine or spruce (chine log)
- ❑ 2 pcs. 3/4" x 1 1/2" x 16' knot free pine or spruce (gunwale)
- ❑ 1 pc. 3/4" x 1 1/2" x 5' vertical grain spruce (frame)
- ❑ 1 pc. 2" x 4" x 5' vertical grain spruce (stems)

Fastenings

- ❑ 1 lb. 7/8" bronze ring nails
- ❑ 50 3/4" #8 bronze slotted head screws
- ❑ 1 lb. 3/4" drywall or deck screws
- ❑ West System epoxy or similar marine epoxy - about 1 quart
- ❑ 10 yards 3" 9 ounce fiberglass tape

Finishing

- ❑ assorted sandpaper
- ❑ oil-based primer
- ❑ semi-gloss enamel (oil or latex)
- ❑ varnish

Note: Paint may also be marine enamel or epoxy.

Seat

- ❑ 1 cane canoe seat or seats can be fabricated

Paddle

- ❑ 1 - 7' or 9' double kayak paddle

Personal Flotation Device

- ❑ 1 PFD/person

Note: Total capacity of boat is approximately 250 lbs. or one adult or two children.

TOOLS:

- ❑ Sliding T-Bevel
- ❑ Square
- ❑ Framing Square
- ❑ 25' Tape Measure
- ❑ 3' Rule
- ❑ Hammer
- ❑ Screwdrivers - Slotted and Phillips
- ❑ Sharp Crosscut Saw
- ❑ Sharp Block Plane
- ❑ Electric Drill and Drill Bits
- ❑ Saber Saw and Sharp Blades
- ❑ 24 2" Spring Clamps
- ❑ 4 12" Bar Clamps

OPTIONAL TOOLS:

- ❑ Band Saw
- ❑ Table Saw
- ❑ Cordless Drill
- ❑ Phillips Bits
- ❑ Random Orbit or Pad Sander
- ❑ Electric Router
- ❑ Flush-Trim Bit for router

B. SUPPLIERS

Below, are listed suppliers of some of the hard-to-find materials used in the boat. Before ordering, however, check with marine dealers in your area to see if materials can be found locally.

Plywood - 1/4" x 4' x 16' Marine Fir

Boulter Plywood Corp.
24 Broadway
Somerville, MA 02145
617-666-1340

Harbor Sales
1401 Russell Street
Baltimore, MD 21230
800-345-1712

Olson Lumber
9300 Aurora North
Seattle, WA 98103
800-533-4381

Bronze Fastenings

Jamestown Distributors
28 Narragansett Avenue
P. O. Box 348
Jamestown, RI 02835
800-423-0030

Epoxy

Gougeon Brothers, Inc.
P. O. Box 908
Bay City, MI 48707
517-684-7286

Systems Three Resins, Inc.
P. O. Box 70436
Seattle, WA 98107
206-782-7976

C. The Butt Block Option

Because it can be expensive to buy and ship sixteen foot long panels of plywood, you may choose to use the "butt block option". This is a way you can use eight foot lengths that can be more easily obtained **and** it opens the possibility of using exterior grade plywood from your local lumber yard if you need to save even more money.

A butt clock is a piece of wood, in this case plywood, that is glued across the joint between two panels to be joined. Here's how it works.

Lay the two panels to be joined on a flat surface and mark the layout lines as indicated in Part I, Section 3. Be sure to mark the position of the frame on the inside and outside of the aft panel. Spring the batten and mark the sheer lines.

Cut out the side panels with a saber saw and trim them to their proper lines. Set the bottom panels aside for now.

Using pieces of scrap plywood, cut three butt blocks: 2 pieces 5" wide by about 10" long for the sides and one piece 5" wide by about 24" long for the bottom. These pieces will be cut to an exact fit as required.

Joining the Sides

Lay the side pieces on a flat surface so they are properly lined up with the **insides** of the panels facing up. Center the 10" long butt block pieces over the joints and mark their positions. Then move the blocks up from the bottom of the panels 1 1/4" and draw a line marking the new position of the bottom of the butt blocks. This new position will allow the proper fitting of the chine logs. Trim off the butt blocks to the proper length. (So they don't stick up above the sheer line.)

Slide a piece of scrap wood, with a piece of waxed paper on top of it, under the joints. This piece should be big enough to provide a backing for the butt block while the pieces are being glued. So pieces at least 5" wide and 10" long should be found. They can be scraps of plywood.

Carefully align the panels and apply epoxy to the areas to be glued, both the panels and the butt blocks. Then position the butt blocks and staple or drive nails through the butt blocks into the scrap wood. Be careful not to get epoxy between the scrap pieces and the panels. Check one last time to see that all is aligned properly and allow to set for 24 hours. When the epoxy has cured, remove the backing blocks and drive out the nails or staples if they protrude.

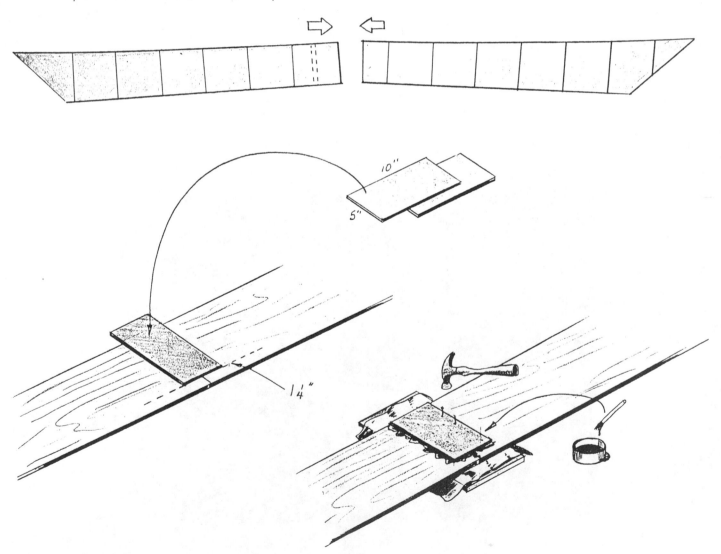

Joining the Bottom Pieces

When you are ready to put the bottom on the boat it is time to mark and apply the butt block to the bottom pieces.

Lay the panels on the bottom of the boat and mark their position. Carefully draw lines marking the outer edge where the bottom meets the sides and on the inside where it meets the chine logs.

Lay the panels on a flat surface with the inside up. Carefully mark the position of the butt block so it fits between the lines marking

the chine logs so the bottom will fit properly when you are ready to attach it to the boat.

Slide a 24" long backer piece and waxed paper under the joint, align the panels and butt block, apply glue and attach as you did with the side panels.

After the epoxy is cured, remove the backer piece and fastenings and you are ready to attach the bottom as described in Part I, Section 13. When attaching the bottom, be sure the butt block fits in between the chine logs so the bottom lays flat on the chine logs.

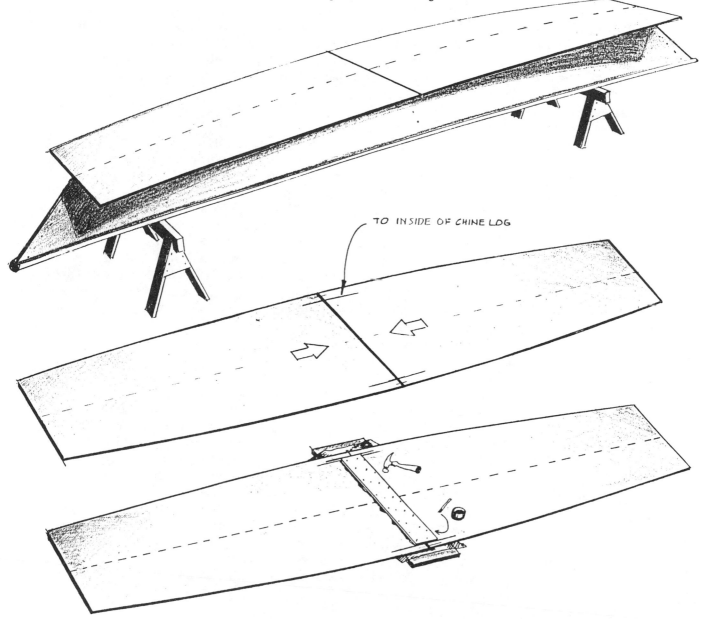

TO INSIDE OF CHINE LOG

Building Canoes And Environmental Awareness

The success of the first printing and the subsequent article in **WoodenBoat** Magazine (July/August, 1995) resulted in over a hundred calls and letters, many from people who were interested in using the Six Hour Canoe in kids' programs. Virtually all of these people lamented the lack of information on successful programs. With that in mind we offer the following which occurred in the fall or 1995.

Waterfront Rediscovery and Kids

Feeling the water lift you as you push off from shore in a boat you built yourself is a powerful experience. That first instant when the momentum of the push off carries you away on the surface of the medium that sustains us all is an instant of elation and wonder that you never forget. Reaching out to touch the water you cannot help but form a personal bond with that medium and in that first experience you have the beginnings of a powerful connection with the aquatic environment.

Now, add junior high school age kids from an inner city neighborhood, a clinic interested in their total health and well being, a college environmental research organization reaching out to the community, a boat building center with an interest in helping kids, community supporters and businesses and you have a coalition for social change and environmental awareness.

Located at the eastern end of Lake Erie, Buffalo is a city that is rediscovering a waterfront that includes the Buffalo and Niagara Rivers and the Erie Barge Canal as well as the lake. Once one of the busiest grain and lumber ports in the world, the waterfront now serves mostly recreational pursuits which have strong interests in a healthy aquatic ecosystem. Those interests can be motivators for environmental education and action.

Living in this waterfront city are kids who have never had access to the water except to chuck a rock or bottle into the river or canal. Serving them is a community health clinic run by Children's Hospital. Recognizing the need to deal with these kids in their family and social context, Peter Winkelstein MD, the director of the clinic, contacted the Center for Watercraft Studies because he had learned of our community outreach programs in which we offered mentored boat building for kids. That contact lead to a successful and ongoing project in which West Side Health Center kids and their families build boats and then use those boats in an environmental awareness program on local waters.

To facilitate aquatic awareness, Mike Weimer a graduate student at the Great Lakes Center for Environmental Research and Education (GLCERE) and I developed a manual of activities including field observations, collecting and lab work that starts with the kids using the boats as "research vessels". Because of its low cost and simplicity of construction, the Six Hour Canoe is an accessible platform from which to take water samples and to collect plankton and other aquatic life.

A Recent Program

Dr. Winkelstein and his staff invited about 10 kids and their families to participate and 6 opted to do so. The selection was based on a variety of needs and the kid's ages ranged from nine to thirteen. Four came from Hispanic backgrounds as the clinic serves a largely Hispanic community. All were economically disadvantaged.

Funding was secured from local businesses which sponsored boats at a cost of $ 250.00 each which paid for materials and incidental expenses such as refreshments and lunches on the two long work days.

College age mentors were recruited and, this time, paid through a grant. But, mentors can be volunteers of any age from seventeen or eighteen.

On the second Saturday in September, the kids and at least one family member arrived at our shop at the college at 9:00 am. Each was introduced to his or her mentor and building materials and the tools necessary to begin building were provided. By noon the boats had begun to take shape and the coveted "inflated rubber glove award" had been made for the "first boat up". By 4:00 PM the boats were ready for their bottoms - the last step.

Sunday at 1:00 PM the participants arrived to glue and nail on the bottoms. They planed and sanded edges and details in preparation for